Allahabad
WHERE THE RIVERS MEET

edited by Neelum Saran Gour
with special photography by Rajesh Vora

Marg publications

The publication of this book has been made possible by generous support received from MOONSAIL LTD and from Chitralekha Pal in memory of Arup Bose and Rakhi Guha

General Editor
PRATAPADITYA PAL
Associate Editor
RASHMI PODDAR

Senior Executive Editor
SAVITA CHANDIRAMANI
Executive Editor
GAYATRI W. UGRA
Senior Editorial Executive
ARNAVAZ K. BHANSALI

Text Editor
RIVKA ISRAEL

Designer
NAJU HIRANI
Senior Production Executive
GAUTAM V. JADHAV
Production Executive
VIDYADHAR R. SAWANT

Vol. 61 No 1
September 2009
Price: Rs 2500.00 / US$ 68.00
ISBN 10: 81-85026-94-7
ISBN 13: 978-81-85026-94-7
Library of Congress Catalog Card Number: 2009-341502

Marg is a registered trademark of Marg Publications
© Marg Publications, 2009
All rights reserved

No part of this publication may be reproduced, stored, adapted, or transmitted, in any form or by any means, electronic, mechanical, photocopying, recording, or otherwise, or translated in any language or performed or communicated to the public in any manner whatsoever, or any cinematographic film or sound recording made therefrom without the prior written permission of the copyright holders.
This edition may be exported from India only by the publishers, Marg Publications, and by their authorized distributors and this constitutes a condition of its initial sale and its subsequent sales.

Published by Radhika Sabavala for Marg Publications
on behalf of the National Centre for the Performing Arts
at 24, NCPA Marg, Nariman Point, Mumbai 400 021.
Processed at Marg, Mumbai 400 001.
Printed at Thomson Press (India) Ltd., Navi Mumbai 400 708.

Captions
Page 1: View of the northern wing of the central Senate House building and the clock tower, Muir College.
Page 2: Sringaverapura ghat on the Yamuna.
Page 3: The Daira-e Sheikh Muhammadi Shah, a Sufi centre and St Thomas Orthodox Syrian Christian Church, Cantonment.
Pages 4–5: A sadhu feeding winter migratory birds on the Sangam against a view of the fort. Courtesy Rajesh Singh.
Pages 6–7: View of Vizianagram Hall and detail of the marble plaque set in the wall beside the east entrance to the Senate Hall, Allahabad University.
Pages 8–9 and endpaper: The Sangam and Kumbh sadhus, illustrations by Durgadatt Pandey.

Marg's quarterly publications receive support from
the Sir Dorabji Tata Trust – Endowment Fund

CONTENTS

8 Map

10 Avatars and Antecedents
Neelum Saran Gour

30 Where Nectar Spilt
Arindam Roy

44 Akbar's Ilahabas
N.R. Farooqi

56 Salim's Taswirkhana
Asok Kumar Das

72 For Company and Queen
John Harrison

86 Vande Bharatam
*Badri Narayan Tiwari
and Neelum Saran Gour*

102 In Eastmancolor
Hemendra Shankar Saxena

114 The Rule of Law
John Harrison

126 Banyan Tree
Manas Mukul Das

138 Prayagvad in Hindi Writing
Harish Trivedi

146 Urdu and Persian Literature
Shamsur Rahman Faruqi

156 Nehru and Later
Gangeya Mukherji

166 A New Triveni
Neelum Saran Gour

178 Index

180 Contributors

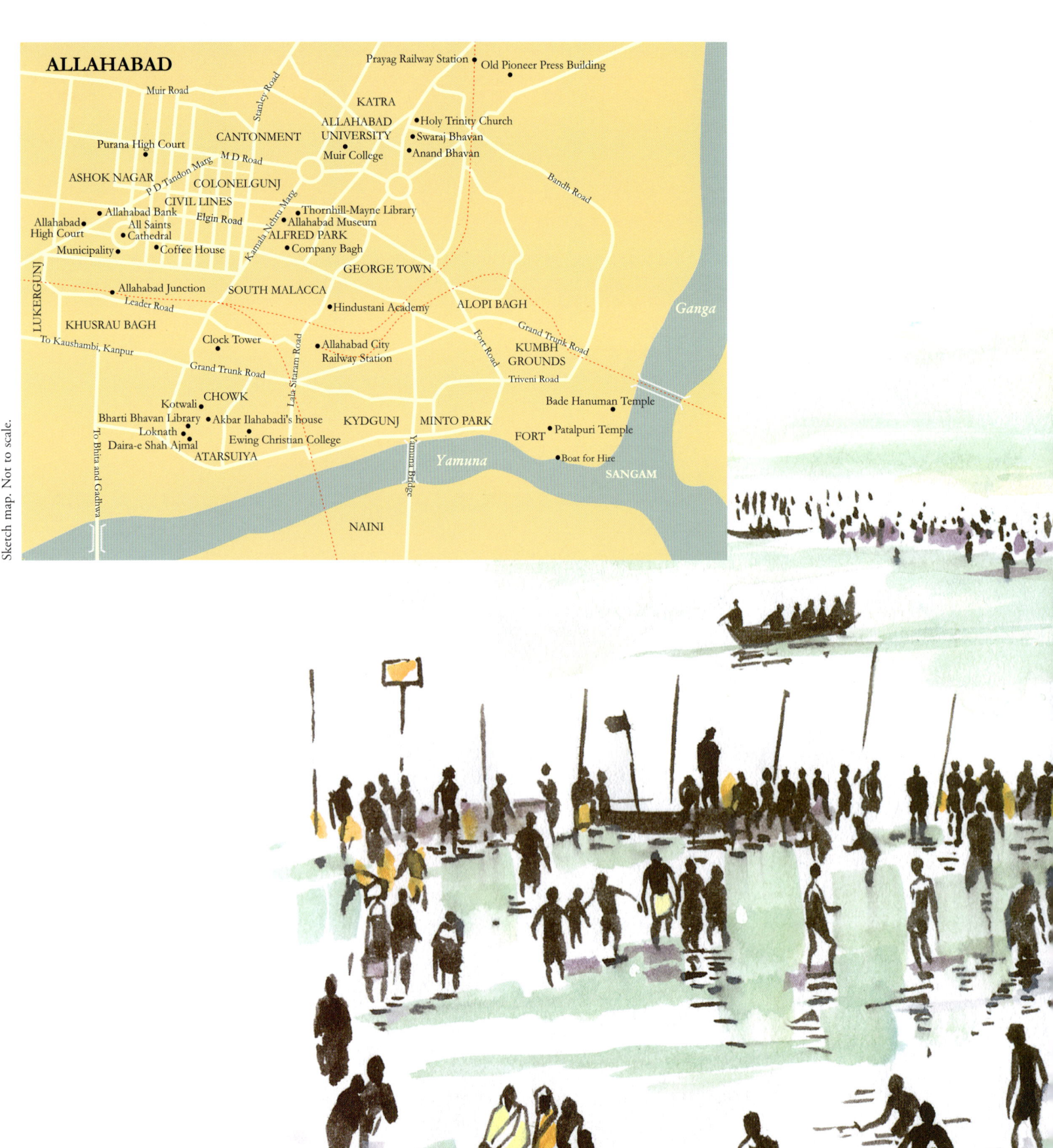

Avatars and Antecedents

Neelum Saran Gour

On a relief map of India the city of Allahabad is like a mustard seed placed exactly where the hairline-blue capillaries of two big rivers meet. Located at the confluence of the Ganga and the Yamuna – in mythological accounts there is a third river, the invisible Saraswati, too – Allahabad has for millennia been a spiritual metropolis for the Hindu world. To the imperial Mughals it held a strategic position for conquest and control. Tavernier claimed that the *subah* (province) of Allahabad was so significant that its governance was conferred only on a son or an uncle of the emperor.[1] And during the Raj it was a prominent administrative hub with a high-profile cultural identity all its own. It enjoyed high political visibility during its hyperactive National Movement days and for decades after 1947 it has been home turf to key national figures. An intermesh of Hindu, Islamic, and British influences, Allahabad supplied a battery of civil servants, jurists, politicians, men of letters, scientists, and academics to the list of India's cutting-edge history-makers. And in the Hindi and Urdu literary space the number of writers groomed by the city is awe-inspiring.

Allahabad abounds in monuments; however its real creative product is not something crafted in a material medium but a kind of intellectual personality – the lawyer, the civil servant, the statesman, and the man of letters – once nurtured in an ambience of aristocratic literary life, upper-crust activism, classy social grace, and high-minded motivation. Long after the ambience was lost, postmodern Allahabad continued to produce personalities in far-flung fields of specialization.

This volume seeks to showcase the many avatars of the city through select sequences of its long and distinguished history. Editing this book has been a pleasure and also a learning experience. For me the city has always registered its character not through impersonal historical accounts but cumulatively through its embedded narratives or *sthal-katha*s, replete with every sort of poetic licence and convenience. There are many more legends than there are monuments. One may regard them as sacred codes, fabular and allegorical constructs, crypto-histories or pseudo-histories, or just culture-gossip – but they have stayed constant in popular memory with a persistence that is enough to merit them the status of non-physical heritage monuments. Allahabad's genius locus, its self-defining essence, lies in these monuments of the imagination, flotsam stories cast upon its riverine banks by the advancing and receding waters of time.

1 *opposite*
Image of Prayagraj, the city apotheosized as a deity, in the Patalpuri Temple.

Antecedents

The rivers scripted the shifting territories of quickening civilization, meandering in wide loops, leaving behind oxbow lakes which slowly silted up to turn into the very first Mesolithic fishing settlements. The first indigenous people migrated northwards from the Kaimur range of the Vindhya mountains, it is calculated, during the 8th millennium BCE. Neolithic locations like Koldihawa bear traces of being among the earliest sites of rice cultivation in the world. Other sites at Sarai Nahar Rai and Mahadaha indicate a state of civilization in the fishing, hunting, and foraging stage. Still earlier Paleolithic remains have been unearthed along the Belan river which flows close to the Mirzapur side on the southeastern end of Allahabad district. The swift-flowing river has cut deep through layered rocks, clearly exposing a cross-section of successive ages from Paleolithic to Neolithic. At Jhunsi, an ancient segment of the city located on the north bank of the Yamuna, Chalcolithic layers diagram a farming civilization, followed by the presence of villages, then evidence of an iron age just prior to the Mahajanapadas and the Mauryas.

Archaeological investigation has established the existence of certain ancient culture clusters scattered around the region encircling the present-day city – a Vatsa here, a Pratishthanpura there, a Bhita, Gadhwa, or Lachchagir close by. These sites excitingly illustrate the numerous ways in which the city has reinvented itself, transmigrating from place to place within a radius of 80 kilometres. Known by many names before it acquired its present one, earlier avatars of the city emerged in a wide belt of riverine territory, more or less culturally continuous, that formed the battleground of many incoming and settled races and the germinating space for evolving creativity.

Using a large array of sources an eventful chronological narrative can be reconstituted, drawing extensively on the evidence of abundant excavated material which includes coins, ceramics, inscriptions, seals, moulds, terracotta figurines, and elaborate monumental remains. Also, plentiful puranic and epic references enhance the authenticated deductions of historians with a mythic dimension. Buddhist and Brahmanical sources and literary cross-references complete the picture which is further sharpened by Chinese and Greek travel accounts. Although Maurya-Sunga-Kushana-Gupta artefacts predominate, a potent Scythian-Parthian-Bactrian-Greek presence is palpable.

Prayag

My special interest has been in the ways in which the folk imagination engages with folk recall to create territorial fables for anthropologists to contextualize and philosophers to decode. And Allahabad, or Prayag, like most cities with a long past, is particularly fertile in this respect.

The *Patal Khand* of the *Padma Purana*, for example, has a 100-verse sequence known as the *Prayag-Mahatmya-Shatadhyayi*. The section holds the answer which Sheshanaga or Vasuki; King of Serpents, who rules the cosmic underworld, gave to the sons of Brahma who had approached him with the question why Prayag, the ancient name for Allahabad, is known as Tirtharaja, king of all places of pilgrimage. Seated on his golden throne, resplendent in his 1,000 hoods and surrounded by *naga*s and *nagini*s, Vasuki told them why the place of king is assigned to Prayag, while

2
Sanctum of the *akshaya-vat*, the famous banyan tree in the underground Patalpuri Temple. On the trunk of the tree is a row of silver masks representing the sons of Brahma.

3
Sanctum of Vasuki, king of the *naga*s, at the Naga-Vasuki Temple. Vasuki rules over the cosmic underworld and recites the *Prayag-Mahatmya-Shatadhyayi*, the 100 verses enumerating the virtues of Prayag in the *Padma Purana*.

eight others – Kashi, Ayodhya, Mathura, Haridwar, Kanchi, Ujjain, Puri, and Dwarka – are the queens. While each of the queens can grant moksha to the pilgrim, the weight of merit to be gained in Prayag outweighs all the rest.

In another story, Prajapati or Brahma wondered which place on earth was the holiest and after intensive meditation chose Prayag. No sooner had he announced his choice than Lord Vishnu, hearing of it, arrived in Prayag in the form of Veni Madhava. Thereupon Brahma performed ten sacrifices, *ashvamedha yajna*s, in Prayag, giving it its name – *pra,* meaning superlative and *yag*, derived from *yajna*. Then Lord Shiva, wishing to have *darshana* of Vishnu, arrived from Kashi and set himself up at the Shultankeshwara Mandir, from which place of vantage he enjoyed constant *darshana* of Lord Vishnu, who sat on the *akshaya-vat* in the form of Bal-Mukund.[2] So, sanctified by the simultaneous presence of all three cosmic personalities of the Hindu trinity, no less than by the confluence of its three rivers, Prayag came to be known as Triveni.

Prayag has sometimes been described as the head of the Cosmic Man, or *Virata-Purusha*, and sometimes the neck, or the feet, or the belly.[3] We are also told that Soma, Varuna, and Prajapati all took birth at Prayag.

In the corpus of ancient and medieval poetry the mingling of the waters at the Sangam has been variously described through a series of expressive conceits. Shankara in the *Saundaryalahari* has compared the confluence of the Ganga, the Yamuna, and the Son (for some peculiar reason replacing the Saraswati) with the white, black, and red hues of the eyes of Shakti. Bilhana, an 11th-century poet at the Chalukyan court, has described the Yamuna plunging into the Ganga as a naked sword plunges into its sheath. And the much quoted lines from Kalidas's poem *Raghuvamsha* has Rama pointing out the Sangam to Sita from the aerial perspective of the *pushpak viman* on their way back from Lanka. The colours of the two streams meeting is like a necklace of pearls set with sapphires; a chaplet of lotuses, white and blue; a row of snowy and dusky swans

14   Neelum Saran Gour

on the Mansarovar lake; a patch of earth adorned with white and dark sandal; moonlight dappled with the shade of leaves; or the blue sky strewn with white clouds. Those who are familiar with the sight of the greenish Yamuna speeding into the silty-white Ganga know exactly what is meant by these lines written by the leading poet of the Gupta period.

Another subject of much puranic lore, which has come to be regarded as the prime emblem of the city is the *akshaya-vat*. Mentioned repeatedly by foreign travellers from Xuanzang (7th century) to Al Biruni (10th–11th century), this ancient banyan tree, enclosed in what is known as the Patalpuri Temple, was said to have been the only thing that survived the last cosmic dissolution or *pralaya*. Having gained a bizarre notoriety as a place of suicide where moksha-seeking pilgrims jumped to their deaths at the *kamya-kup* or wish-granting well, the *akshaya-vat* and Patalpuri Temple were enclosed and Akbar's fort was built around them for situational and policy reasons.

4
View of the Naga-Vasuki Temple on the bank of the Ganga. Every year, on Naga Panchami, crowds of snake-charmers swarm to the temple which is sacred to Vasuki, king of serpents.

AVATARS AND ANTECEDENTS

5
The recumbent Hanuman at the Bade Hanumanji Mandir, Allahabad's best-known temple on the Ganga sands. The image is submerged by the flood waters of the swollen Ganga each monsoon. Local lore has mythologized this phenomenon and spun a fable about the Ganga coming annually to touch Hanuman's feet in worship.

6
Sanctum of the Alopi Devi Temple, Allahabad, a *siddha-peeth* sacred to the devi and the scriptural site where a finger of the devi is believed to have fallen when the grief-maddened Shiva stormed across the universe carrying her dead and disintegrating body. The temple is frequented by women and is remarkable in possessing no icon in the main sanctum. Instead, a swinging cradle serves as the receptacle for offerings and oblations. The temple was the rallying ground for Indian sepoys in 1857.

7
Temple at Sringaverapura on the Ganga, mythological site where the exiled Rama is said to have crossed the river on his way to the forest.

AVATARS AND ANTECEDENTS

17

8
View of the mound known as *ulta qila* or upside-down citadel at Jhunsi. The name Jhunsi has etymological links with the Hindi word *jhulasna* or *jhulasa* which means "scorched". An important archaeological site, the name suggests the occurrence of some natural disaster of magnitude unrecorded in official history.

Pratishthanpura

Arcane stories and archaeological excavations equally contribute to the antique personality of the city, the narrative lines blurring inevitably into a mythological mist. Jhunsi or Pratishthanpura on the north bank of the Yamuna is said to have been established by King Pururava of the lunar race, the Primeval Man, *Purva-Purusha*, grandson of Manu-Vaivasvata. His mother Ila's name may have something to do with Allahabad's earlier name, Ilahabas. Nahush, Yayati, Dushyant, and Bharat are all supposed to have reigned from Pratishthanpura. There is also the greatly enigmatic story of the *ulta qila*, the inverted citadel of the "*andher nagari – chaupat raja*", which roughly translates as "king of a dark, preposterous city of a messed-up kingdom", which bears the clouded traces of some episode of primeval devastation that overtook the kingdom. Even today in Jhunsi villagers and children recount some garbled account of an absurd ruler of an absurd kingdom divorced from all common sense.

Kaushambi

In the case of Kaushambi (Kosam), 60 kilometres away and situated on the left bank of the Yamuna, virtual and actual history combine to unfold a breathtaking picture of a highly developed, dominant, and enduring civilization that existed long before the commencement of the Common Era. Its origins are variously suggested. A flourishing capital city of the kingdom of Vatsa at the time of the *Upanishads* (c. 6th century BCE), the founding of the city is ascribed in the *Mahabharata* to the third son of Uparichar Vasu of the Chedi dynasty, Kushamb by name. The *Ramayana,* however, attributes the city's founding to an ancient king named Kush. But the most popular account lies in the *Matsya Purana* which describes how the Ganga rose and flooded Hastinapur, forcing King Nichakshu (of the house of Bharat), fifth in line after Arjuna's grandson, Parikshit, to relocate to Kaushambi.[4] Pali sources trace the origins of the city to the ashram of a rishi named Kosamba, and the 6th-century Buddhist writer Buddhaghosa asserts that the city got its name from the thousands of Kosambha

(Kusum, *Schleichera oleosa*) trees which were uprooted in order to build it. Whatever the truth of its origin, the village of Kosam has provided posterity with abundant archaeological material to keep historians busy for generations.

From various accounts we know that at the time of the Buddha, Vatsa-desha, of which Kaushambi was the capital, was a prosperous *janapada* among the 16 major *janapada*s of north India, and one of the six metropolises of the period. We also know that Kaushambi, at the height of its power, was one of the most important Buddhist centres in north India; that the Buddha visited Kaushambi in the sixth and ninth years after his enlightenment; that Udayan Vatsa, the famous king, converted to Buddhism; and that Ghoshil, an important minister and Buddha's disciple, built the Ghoshitarama Vihara where the Buddha stayed, preached, and oversaw the functioning of the Sangha.

To the art historian, Kaushambi's excavated treasures are a window to the sophisticated civilization which produced them.[5] Early ceramic samples belonging to the period 600 BCE to 400 CE carry a profusion of geometrical designs, horizontal and vertical stripes, checks, rectangles with inset circles, floral motifs, decorative wheels, oblong petals, stylized pipal leaves, lotus patterns, and scrolls. There are also what are known as *makaramukha* spouts and handles on vessels belonging to the Saka (Scythian)-Kushana era. The figure of the bull dominates both sculpture and coins.

9
Ruins at Bhita, identified as the lost city of Beethbhayapattan. The shrine located on a rock is sacred to Hindus, Buddhists, and Muslims, an interesting example of historical ambiguity, overlap, and adaptability.

Avatars and Antecedents   19

A rare double-humped camel image is believed to point at a possible connection with Bactria. Maurya-Sunga ruins of monuments similar to those at Sanchi and Bharhut have also been found – stupas, pillars, architraves – along with images of buddhas, bodhisattvas, and folk deities, as also repeated symbols of the swastika, the tree-within-a-railing, the lotus, the lion, the palm-leaf, the *triratna*, the *srivatsa*, the *nagapushpa*, the *purnaghata*. The figure of Gajalakshmi (a form of Lakshmi with ornate and elevated headgear crowned by a tiara, and two elephants producing a cascade of water that washes her form) occurs on coins as well as on pillars, architraves, and relief panels, and is special to Kaushambi. An interesting speculation is that she symbolizes the land itself, washed by the two rivers. A palm-leaf capital of the Sunga period appears to have connections with the Bhagavata cult, indicating a concurrent non-Buddhist presence in the kingdom. Ruins of a palace complex, thought to be Udayan's, and elaborate encircling defence mounds remain. The picture is fleshed out by the accounts of Faxian (early 5th century) and Xuanzang, both of whom visited Kaushambi and recorded their impressions of the metropolis.

Under Udayan's weak successors, Vatsa-desa was conquered by the Nandas of Magadha and in turn annexed to the Maurya empire by Chandragupta Maurya in 321 BCE. Ashoka's pillar which earlier stood at Kaushambi (and is now within the Fort) is one of the most eloquent representations of Maurya – and Buddhist – pre-eminence. After the Mauryas the Sungas under Pushyamitra overran the region. There are also many evidences of the presence of the Yavanas or Bactrian Greeks. Arrowheads belonging to the period between 255 and 185 BCE have been found at Kaushambi and it is believed that the Yavana general, Demetrius, attacked the kingdom in the 2nd century BCE. The Hellenization of names on coins – names ending in "us" – is matched by the occurrence of names ending in "mitra", both pointing at an interesting absorption of external influences, before the region was swept into the Kushana empire under Kanishka in 80 BCE. Although Kanishka espoused Buddhism, the Scythian-

10
Ashoka's pillar at Kaushambi.

NEELUM SARAN GOUR

11
Remains of the *janapada* of Vatsa at Kaushambi.

12
The temple at Gadhwa, identified as the ancient Gupta city of Bhattagram.

Avatars and Antecedents

21

Parthian presence is obvious. Once Kushana power diminished, the Maghas, a local dynasty with its base at Bandhavgarh (now in Madhya Pradesh), took control in 155 CE and ruled until overthrown by Samudragupta, the conquering, empire-building Gupta.

The imperial Guptas have left abundant marks of their artistic excellence in the area, especially at Gadhwa, identified as the ancient Gupta city of Bhattagram, where inscriptions from the reigns of Chandragupta II and Kumaragupta, belonging to circa 406–486 CE have been unearthed. Gadhwa has a fort-like structure and a temple with beautifully carved door jambs and lintels. Both nearby Bhita (which Alexander Cunningham in 1872 identified as the lost city of Beethbhayapattan that had flourished at the time of Mahavira) and Jhunsi have a wealth of archaeological material from Gupta times. The ivory coins of Bhita are especially interesting. What is still more exciting is that coins with the name of the Hun conqueror Toramana have also been found at Kaushambi and we now know that the Huns dealt a crushing blow to the kingdom some time between 510 and 515 CE from which Kaushambi never recovered. And although Yashodharman (533–534) did defeat the Huns soundly, Kaushambi became a subservient satellite power, passing into the possession of the kings of Kanauj.

Harsha and After

The most famous of the Kanauj kings, Harshavardhana, was specially associated with Prayag because of his religious conferences on the banks of the Sangam in the month of Magh every year, an event made famous by Xuanzang's graphic account. The liberality with which the king gave away all his accumulated wealth to the poor and holy of three religions – Buddhists, Shaivites, and sun-worshippers – has become a theme of catholicity in the city's collective memory. Harsha ruled till 647 CE. Towards the close of the 8th century the region was occupied and administered by the Gurjara-Pratiharas, particularly the kings Vatsaraja (783–784) and Nagabhatta (815–833). The predatory Rashtrakutas, under their ruler Indra III, invaded the province in 916 but did not stay or settle. The Chandela king, Dhang, however, occupied the area between 950 and 1008 and is said to have voluntarily chosen death by immersion in the holy Sangam at achieving a hundred years of age. The last of the Pratiharas ruled over a shrunken empire, driven back by the onslaught of Mahmud Ghaznavi and reduced to being local rajas. For a brief while a Kalachuri raja, Gangeyadeva, controlled Prayag a little before 1041; he is said to have died in the city along with his hundred wives! His descendants were worsted by the powerful Gahadawala Rajputs, who dominated the province till the armies of Muhammad Ghori overthrew and slew their best-known ruler, Jaichand of Kanauj, towards the close of the 12th century.

Under the Sultanates the administrative locus shifted 65 kilometres northwest along the Ganga to a new urban centre at Kara-Manikpur, Indo-Turk capital of the *subah* for the next three centuries.

Ilahabas

It fell to the great Mughal Akbar (r. 1556–1605) to build a new city. His biographer, Abul Fazl records the Emperor's fervent wish to locate this city beside the confluence, a spot sacred to the country's sadhus and sanyasins. Akbar, who officialized the name

13
Streets illuminated for the Ram-dal procession. Courtesy Anand Srivastava, Photo-journalism Department, Allahabad University.

14
Decorated floats in the Ram-dal procession. Courtesy Anand Srivastava, Photo-journalism Department, Allahabad University.

Ilahabas (the transition to Allahabad is unclear), is surely the story-maker's favourite personality. Local Akbar-lore ideates beyond the known and freewheels as a separate category of popular mythology. There is the legend of Mukund Brahmachari, a hermit who lived on the bank of the Yamuna near the *akshaya-vat* and who inadvertently swallowed a bit of cow's hair in the milk he drank. This being tantamount to eating beef, he agonized on the defilement and his irreversible descent into the ranks of the *mlechcha*s. To atone he leapt from the *akshaya-vat* into the river, in his last moments desiring to be reborn as a "Mussalman emperor of Hindustan". His loyal servant, though personally undefiled, followed suit in sheer solidarity. Mukund, it is said, was reborn as Akbar, his servant as Birbal and, as ordained by the logic of reincarnation, they transmigrated to the site of their former lives where Akbar built his fort, obeying the promptings of his

15
Rama, Lakshmana, and Sita. A gorgeously lit up *chowki* or float in the traditional Patharchatti Ram-dal. Courtesy Anand Srivastava, Photo-journalism Department, Allahabad University.

transcendental memory, and Birbal, the counsellor and court wit, became closely associated with Allahabad.

When Akbar arrived in the city in 1580 many local rajas visited him to offer *nazrana*. Only the Raja of Jhunsi was bashful, not having anything valuable enough to take to the royal audience. His trusty minister (who in this story was Birbal) came up with a quirky idea: he made his raja arrange a silver sledge-hammer and some Ganga sand on a silver platter with tulsi leaves and flowers, and take it to the emperor. Perplexed, the emperor asked what the strange gifts meant. Birbal replied that his raja was obliquely suggesting that Akbar should use his land to build a fort, the gifts being puja items for the foundation-laying ceremony.

One might be disposed to dismiss local lore as classic pseudo-history but popular stories such as these arise from an imaginative field nourished by collective ethnic attitudes. It is significant that these Akbar-centric tales are Hindu narratives, assimilating the persona of a popular Muslim ruler into the Hindu idiom of belonging, using the convenient narrative device of rebirth. Akbar continues to rule in popular memory. An elderly Ramlila artiste of the Jadia community claims that his ancestors came to Allahabad during Akbar's reign and worked as brocade-makers in the fort.[6] Also that the emperor loved Ramlilas and once even lent a shoulder to carry Sitaji's *palki*, and donated land to the Patharchatti Ramlila Committee by a royal *farman*.

Ramkathas

Which brings me to Allahabad's most popular performance art. The Ramkathas or Ramlilas of Allahabad have been famous for centuries, being a ten-day folk dramatization of the *Ramayana* followed by glittering processions of tableaux on wheels, the Ramdals, a day allotted to each area of the city to have its mela and its procession. There are stories behind this tradition too. Each year, in the month of Magh [the time of the Kumbh Mela in January–February], recounts Tulsidas, a congregation of sages used to gather at the hermitage of the sage Bharadwaja for philosophic discourse and dips in the holy Ganga, which then flowed right behind the ashram. One particular year, as the revered guests were

16
Lord Rama and Guha, the king of the Nishadas. An episode in a Ramlila performance. Courtesy Anand Srivastava, Photo-journalism Department, Allahabad University.

17
Rama, Lakshmana, and Sita leaving for the forest. A scene in a Ramlila performance. Courtesy Anand Srivastava, Photo-journalism Department, Allahabad University.

AVATARS AND ANTECEDENTS

leaving, the host clasped the feet of the illustrious Yajnavalkya and begged him to stay on and narrate the story of Sri Rama, which Yajnavalkya graciously did. Ever after, Ramkathas have been enacted during Dasehra in the city of Prayag.[7]

Rama himself is credited with having visited Prayag twice, once on his way to the forest (at Bharadwaja Ashram there is an annual fair commemorating the meeting of Rama and Bharata) and once on his victorious return from Lanka when he is said to have done penance for the sin of killing Ravana, a twice-born brahmin, by installing a crore Shiva-lingas at Shivkoti, a ghat on the Ganga. Another famous ghat on the Ganga, Sringaverapura, is associated with Rama's forestward advance, being the spot where the king of the Nishadas, Guha, rowed him across the river, a specially tender episode in the *Ramayana*. Sringaverapura is also an important historic site and a source of more valuable archaeological material.

By contrast the *Mahabharata* is less physically represented but there is a site called Lakshagriha in the village of Bharot in Handia, a tehsil of Allahabad (also famous as the original home of little-known Kathak teachers of well-known Kathak maestros of the Banaras, Lucknow, and Jaipur schools) where a mound is said to represent the site of the palace of lac in which Duryodhana attempted to trap and burn the wandering Pandavas. The village is also said to be the home of Hidimba, Bhima's ogress wife, in popular tradition. The city has a ghat and a tiny temple to Draupadi as well.

The Ram-dals of Allahabad are spectacular displays, especially the rival Patharchatti and Pajawa processions taken out in the heart of Chowk Gangadas. Since the 19th century these have been traditionally sponsored by the wealthy Khatri merchant-bankers of Rani Mandi. Moneylenders to British officers and Indian princes, dealers in indigo and brocade,

18
Relief depicting Rama, Lakshmana, and their monkey friends. Sringaverapura, 5th century. Courtesy Allahabad Museum.

19 *opposite*
Statue of King Harsha, the bountiful, situated near the Magh Mela grounds. The annual fair held in the month of Magh on the extensive riverside grounds, dates back to the reign of Harshavardhana of Kanauj and has been described in detail by Xuanzang. The generous king Harsha gave away all his worldly goods in charity to the poor and holy of three religious faiths – even the clothes he wore – until he stood clad only in his loincloth, after which he was ritually offered a robe by his sister Rajyashree.

NEELUM SARAN GOUR

designers of fabulous costumes for rajas, chieftains (*raees*es), and famous courtesans and dancers, these local *mahajan*s were co-founders of the Allahabad Bank and owners of vast properties in the city. They sponsored the building of the Chowk clock-tower, designed by Sir Swinton Jacob, and they were connoisseurs of gems, horses, and antiques. They were especially fond of Holi, Janmashtami, and Ram-dal festivities. Many of them, dressed in gorgeous, princely attire, personally accompanied the Ram-dals on their horses or elephants. The line of horses and elephants often used to be several kilometres long. Lala Manohar Das, Lala Manmohan Das (or Bachcha-ji), Babu Dwarkanath "Gotewale", Lala Anandi Lal, Lala Mishri Lal, Lala Lakshminarain, all the legendary capitalists and financiers of Chowk were great patrons of the classic north Indian Hindu festivals. Some like Bachcha-ji happily lent his buggy horses for the Muharrram *dul-dul* as well. Babu Dwarkanath's Janmashtamis were sumptuous affairs for which the uncannily gifted toy-maker, Ali Hussain, fashioned perfect marvels in clay. And the great Holi extravaganzas of Chowk were hosted by the glamorous young Lala Lakshminarain who loved horse-racing. He introduced nationalist themes in the Ram-dal tableaux. At his Holi celebrations *itr, tesu*-flower dye, rose- and *kewra*-water were splashed on guests and the choicest sweets and *thandai* were on offer.[8] Poetry festivals of a riotous kind were, and continue to be, special Holi features.

Festivities were dear to the merchant-bankers' hearts, so much so that when the great exhibition of 1911 was held at Allahabad in which the first aeroplanes in India were on display, and the first air courier service in the world took off from Allahabad to Naini, Lala Vishveshvardas sent the aristocratic ladies of his family, who otherwise stayed decorously at home, to witness these incredible *pushpak viman*s they knew from their *Ramayana*s.

I once had the chance to meet the members of a peasant Ramlila troupe which called itself the Jai Ma Mandavi Devi Ramlila Mandal. Farmers round the year and travelling actors in the Dasehra season, they came forward to introduce themselves to me. Santosh Kumar Mishra acted Rama. Brijesh

Kumar Mishra did Lakshmana. Ajay Kumar Saroj made a lithe, coy Sita. Hanuman humorously showed me his detachable and portable tail, the same tail that had set Lanka aflame onstage the previous evening, and told me his name was Shukru Lal. There was also Baburam, who did Shurpanakha and Meghnad both. Ravana, who sat on a *charpai* with his chillum, was a man of enormous dignity. Years of roaring onstage had affected his voice, and when compelled to speak low he produced odd wheezes and strained growls. His name was Shukradev Chaube. They had, they said, been acting the story of Rama since they were children, playing a Ramlila game on the sly, creating a makeshift stage out of old saris and burning bicycle tyres to produce lighting. Often they forgot to come home for meals and were soundly thrashed by their parents. Then came the unforgettable day when they stole money to buy a *Ramacharitmanas*. "The book is our guru," they told me, "and we keep it garlanded." Five thousand rupees was what they made in season, after which they went back to the fields. Then one, who was called the "harmonium-master" rippled his keys, plied the bellows, and sang me some parts of the forthcoming performance. The verses with their sublime, rural sweetness, seemed to come from a long way off, a long time back. Very like the Ganga, seen of a morning from Phaphamau Bridge – sandy, moonstone-pale, and silvered over with light.

NOTES

1   Surendra Nath Sinha, *Subah of Allahabad Under The Great Mughals*, Jamia Millia Islamia, New Delhi, 1974, p. 89.

2   Jagdish Gupta, "*Prayag ki Garima aur Itihas*", *Prayag, Ateet, Vartaman aur Bhavishya* (in Hindi), edited by Badri Narayan and Y.P. Singh, Vani Prakashan, Allahabad, 2003, pp. 9–10.

3   Deen Bandhu Pandey, "Interesting References to the Anthropomorphic Form of Prayag", *Triveni*, edited by D.P. Dubey and Neelam Singh, The Society of Pilgrimage Studies, Allahabad, 1995, p. 10.

4   The *U.P. Gazetteer*, 1966, reprint 1986, pp. 12–20.

5   Pushpa Tiwari, "Kaushambi: The Glorious Art Centre of Prayag Mandal", *Triveni*, 1995, pp. 22–29.

6   *Hindustan Times*, *Allahabad Live*, October 17, 2007.

21
Indian Posts' first-day cover commemorating the world's first-ever air courier service, from Allahabad to Naini, 1911. Courtesy H.S. Saxena.

7   Surendra Singh Chauhan, "*Prayag Men Ramkatha*", *Prayag, Ateet, Vartaman aur Bhavishya*, pp. 108–09.

8   B.S. Gehlot, *Ilahabad – Ve Din, Ve Log* (in Hindi), Raka Prakashan, Allahabad, pp. 270–302.

ACKNOWLEDGEMENTS

For granting permission for photography, for generously sharing artefacts, the resources of archives and extensive information, for advice and valuable guidance, grateful thanks are due to:

- The Allahabad Museum
- The Indian Army
- Anand Bhavan
- The Allahabad High Court Museum
- The Allahabad University
- The Department of Photo-journalism, Allahabad University
- The Archaeological Survey of India
- Teen Murti Bhavan, New Delhi

This volume has been put together with the cooperation of many people. I would like to thank: Dhananjay Chopra for arranging the Ramlila and Ram-dal images; Sanjay Garg for sharing an image of Akbar's Ilahabas coin; the swamis of the Naga Vasuki, Mankameshwar, and Alopi Devi Temples and Swami Anandgiri of the Hanuman Temple; Jata Shankar Shukla for organizing the temple photography; S.K. Sharma, Sunil Gupta, and Rajesh Mishra of the Allahabad Museum for their advice and knowledgeable instructions; Colonels Roy and Chandel of the Indian Army's Allahabad division for arranging and facilitating our photography session in the Allahabad Fort; Brigadier Rakesh Nandan for securing permission for photography from the Army Headquarters in New Delhi; S.P. Mall and Pramod K. Pandey of Anand Bhavan for organizing our photo-shoots there; John and Anne Harrison for sending valuable archival images of Allahabad city; Justice Ravi Dhawan and Lucinda Dhawan for advice on photo-sites and angles; Justice Sunil Ambwani for personally facilitating photography in the Allahabad High Court; the staff of the Allahabad High Court Museum, especially Mr Ahad, for their help; the staff of the Hindustani Academy; the Principal of the Yaadgar-e Husaini College; the *sajjadanasheen*s of the Daira-e Sheikh Muhibbullah Shah, the Daira-e Sheikh Muhammadi, and the Daira-e Shah Ajmal; Devanshu Gour for ably assisting in the choice of locations and in the photography itself; Amitanshu Gour for taking care of all computer-related jobs; Sudhanshu Gour for being actively involved in the conceptualization of the text.

Finally I express my gratitude to Marg Publications, and all the contributors of text and photographs without whose participation this volume would not have been possible.

20 *opposite*
Temple at Bharadwaja Ashram, located at the site of sage Bharadwaja's hermitage mentioned in the *Ramayana*. An annual fair is held nearby to commemorate the meeting between Rama and his brother, Bharat, who came from Ayodhya to implore Rama to return to the throne, but instead was compelled to go back carrying Rama's sandals. The fair is held a few days after Divali and is called the Bharat Milap ka Mela. Bharadwaja Ashram is also the site where Yajnavalkya is said to have retold the story of Lord Rama.

1
Priestly elders of the Nirvani sect performing their rituals at the Kumbh. Courtesy Rajesh Singh.

Where Nectar Spilt

Arindam Roy

Mythological time and historical chronology may not be contiguous or of equal dimensions, but they interlock and overlap in popular imagination at the Kumbh Mela at Prayag every 12 years, when Allahabad becomes one of the most crowded places on earth during this great bathing festival in the Hindu month of Magh (January–February). Hindus believe that bathing at the confluence of the three rivers, the Ganga, Yamuna, and the invisible Saraswati, especially at this time, frees them from the karmic cycle of birth and death.

Genesis of the Kumbh Mela

The genesis of this festival lies in the myth of the Samudra Manthan, the Churning of the Ocean of Milk which ensued when the *deva*s (gods), enfeebled by the constant and unremitting onslaughts of the *asura*s (demons), approached Brahma, the Creator, who advised them to seek Vishnu's counsel. On Vishnu's advice the gods made a pact with the demons to undertake together the task of Churning the Ocean of Milk and divide the nectar equally between them.

A hill, Mandara, was used as the churning stick, while the king of serpents, Vasuki, was used as the rope. Vishnu himself took the form of Kurma the tortoise, on whose back the stick rested. After ages of churning, fumes, gases, fire, and deadly poison came forth. In order to spare the world, Lord Shiva drank the poison, as no gods or demons were ready to risk their lives.

Soon 14 precious gifts surfaced, among them a flying horse, a legendary cow, a priceless jewel, the magic moon, a sky chariot, Rambha (the beautiful apsaras), Lakshmi (the consort of Vishnu), and Vishwakarma (the divine architect). At last, Dhanvantari, the divine healer, surfaced with a *kumbha* or pot containing the nectar.

Once they had the nectar, the gods, as they had secretly decided, declined to share it with the demons. Quarrels broke out. So Vishnu took the form of a beautiful woman, Mohini, to seduce the demons and divert their attention from the nectar, allowing Jayant, the son of Indra, to escape with the pot. Jayant rested at 12 places, of which four were on the earth, while eight were in the heavens (*devalok*). The earthly stops were Prayag, Haridwar, Ujjain, and Nasik. Some drops of the nectar fell at each of these places, sanctifying them. That is why the Kumbh is held, by rotation, once every 12 years at each of these *tirth*s.

2 *above*
Ceremonial fanfare at the Kumbh. Courtesy Rajesh Singh.

3 *left*
Pilgrims resting on the sandy riverbank on a foggy Magh morning. Courtesy Rajesh Singh.

4 *top*
Warrior-ascetics of the Naga sect perform incredible acrobatic feats. Courtesy Rajesh Singh.

5 *below*
This "baba" has mastered the skill of circling in the water for long stretches of time, balancing a pot on his head. Courtesy Rajesh Singh.

Other parallel stories circum-narrate the basic myth, replacing characters and shuffling episodes but keeping to the essence of the story. Two variants proceed thus: When Sage Durvasa, the angry one, offered a garland to Indra, the latter committed the unforgivable offence of crowning his elephant Airavata's head with it. And Airavata, tossing his head, threw the garland to the ground and trampled on it. Enraged, Durvasa cursed the world with drought and colossal natural disasters. Hence the Samudra Manthan became necessary. In this version the *asura*s cheated and ran away with the pot of nectar. They hid it in their serpent-domain beneath the world, and it fell to Garuda to retrieve the pot and carry it back to the Ocean of Milk. He too spilt nectar at the same four places, which became sites for Kumbh Melas.

Another version recounts how the two co-wives of Prajapati Kashyap, Kadru and Vinta, laid a wager on whether the Sun's horses were black or white. Vinta lost because Kadru's sons, the *naga*s, obscured the Sun and made the horses appear black. As decided, Vinta was reduced to servitude to Kadru for life. Vinta made a bid for freedom by asking her son, Garuda, to bring her the pot of nectar guarded by Vasuki in the underworld. Garuda successfully did this, fending off attacks from the *naga*s and resting the pot in four places.

The *Veda*s, *Purana*s, the epics *Ramayana* and *Mahabharata*, and the Tantra texts abound with references to the Kumbh. Vedic hymns indicate the spiritual significance of the Kumbh. In the *Purana*s, the Kumbh has been mentioned as a holy time for the performance of death rites on the banks of the Saraswati where also a holy dip is believed to bestow the benefits of performing a *yajna*. The *Mahabharata, Agni Purana, Padma Purana*, and *Surya Purana* also mention Prayag as the holiest of all places of pilgrimage.

Planetary conjunction plays an important role in deciding the timing of the Kumbh Mela once in every 12 calendar years. The transition of Jupiter, along with the positions of the Sun and Moon, are the most important factors, according to the Hindu almanac, in deciding the timing of the Kumbh Mela at the four *tirtha*s. As explicated in the ancient texts: *Magh Mesh Gatey Jive / Makare Chandra Bhaskaro*, when Jupiter is in Aries in the month of Magh, while the Sun and Moon are in Capricorn, [the Kumbh occurs at Prayag].

Significance of the Kumbh Mela

This age-old festival fulfilled various functions. Ideally it was an occasion for sages to congregate and deliberate on the well-being of the world and share their enlightenment with ordinary humanity. The Kumbh Mela has traditionally also provided the opportunity for sages and rulers to establish communication. The cycle congregating at four places over 12 years meant that these people, who virtually controlled the socio-religious order of ancient India, met once every three years. Other than the Kumbh Mela, an in-between cycle of meeting also took place at two places, Allahabad and Haridwar, which came to be known as Ardh Kumbh (once in six years at each place).

The chill sands of the river banks play host to searching discourses on the self, the meaning of life, and the nature of the divine. The fair serves as an occasion for interreligious consensus and exchange. Above all it forms a platform for Hindu religion and spirituality. There are also discourses on the preservation of the environment and a showcasing of Indian cultural richness.

6 *opposite*
Chanting mantras to the holy Ganga, this sadhu has a ritual bath in its waters at the Sangam.

7
A Naga procession by night. The Nagas (not to be confused with Vasuki or his serpent subjects) are a sect of ascetic warriors founded by Adi Shankaracharya. They wear no clothes, are extremely fierce, and excel in difficult yogic feats. Courtesy Rajesh Singh.

There is a folk entertainment aspect too. The grand processions and *shahi snan* (regal bath) of the Naga sadhus and other seers, which continue to this day, often on a very grand scale, might be compared to modern-day carnivals. Then there are plays based on religious themes, with actors (*bahurupiya*s) dressed up as the monkey-god Hanuman and indulging in hilarious pranks, or appearing as other gods and demons. *Pravachan*s (discourses), *kirtan*s (singing of devotional verses), *havan*s (offerings to appease gods), *go-daan* (cow-offerings), and *shraddha* (obsequies), along with *kalpavas* (ascetic retreat), are the highlights of the Kumbh.

Kumbh Processions

The various sects of the Naga sadhus (Hindu militants organized by Adi Shankaracharya in the 8th century to check the threat of Buddhists and other sects) begin with the Mauni Amavasya Snan. They come out in a particular order. The sect leaders, Mahamandaleshwars (next to the Shankaracharyas), Mandaleshwars, and

Acharyas are seated on decorated thrones, atop elephants or tractor trolleys. Each sect has its flag, much like an army regiment. The hair arrangements and sandalwood *tilaka*s on their foreheads are intricate. After the *shahi snan* by the sadhus, the ordinary devotees bathe in the rivers.

The Nagas are naked sadhus, who smear themselves with ashes. Their matted hair, bloodshot eyes (a result of smoking marijuana in chillums or mud pipes), and faces smeared with vermilion and sandalwood paste give them a wild look. Some of them ride horses and engage in sword fights, en route to the Sangam. Bands of musicians accompany them, as pilgrims stand with folded hands, unmindful of their gross nudity. Vaishnava, Shaiva, Shakta, Yoga, Mimamsa, Sankhya – all Hindu sects and orders – have a presence at the Kumbh. Their names have a resonance of centuries of *sadhana* and *sankalpa*, of spiritual as well as temporal command: Mahanirvani (Shaiva, with matted locks), Niranjani (naked Shaivas with matted locks), Baghambari

8
Devotees at a sect-camp, or *akhara*, seated at a community meal. Courtesy Rajesh Singh.

9
A local citizen dresses up as Santa Claus and distributes sweets to pilgrims at the Sangam. Courtesy Rajesh Singh.

(Shaivas without matted locks), Ramanuji (Vaishnavas), followers of Vallabha, Nimbarka, Madhavacharya, Chaitanya, Radhavallabhi, Ramanandi, Panchayati Udaaseen, Nirvani Udaaseen, Chhota Panchayati Udaaseen.

Kalpavas

The word *kalpa* means transformation of the self by inner resolve, and *vas* means living out this resolve. The single-minded pursuit of this great inner change is the object of *kalpavas*. During the six-week Kumbh Mela, *kalpavasi*s inhabit an extensive temporary city of thatched huts and tents that spring up on the banks of the Sangam with meticulous local planning. The *kalpavasi*s are mostly drawn from villages all over India, however urban dwellers along with sadhus and ascetics of different Hindu sects also make up the population of the Kumbh Mela. Foreign visitors, looking for the exotic or seeking spiritual options, also abound. Social scientists studying the workings of peaceful coexistence have participated as well – for example the scholars from St Andrew's University, Scotland, at the 2006 Ardh Kumbh who made interesting findings on harmonious living. Musicians of national standing perform and exhibitions on various subjects are organized here.

The *kalpavasi*s spend the six-week period on the river banks leading an austere life. They sleep on straw, listen to discourses, and give alms. They bathe thrice daily and eat only once in 24 hours. Some devotees opt for shorter periods of *kalpavas,* ranging from three or five days to a month.

The *Vishnu Purana* states that the benefit from bathing during the Kumbh is equal to performing 1,000 *ashwamedha yajna*s (horse sacrifices) or circumambulating the earth 10 lakh times. It is said that by bathing at the Kumbh Mela not only are one's own sins washed away but that 88 generations of one's ancestors are benefited as well.

Accounts of the Kumbh

It is said that Megasthenes, the Greek ambassador to the court of Chandragupta Maurya, visited the Kumbh Mela for 75 days, in the 4th century BCE. Later, in the 7th century CE, the Chinese pilgrim Xuanzang toured India. He visited Prayag and mentioned the great Mela, recording the benevolence of King Harshavardhana at Prayag who came here after a gap of five years and gave away all his belongings to ascetics and the poor until he was reduced to the barest loincloth. According to some scholars, this marked the beginning of the Ardh Kumbh.

The American writer Mark Twain could hardly contain his wonder, when he wrote in his book *More Tramps Abroad* (1895), "These pilgrims had come from all over India: some of them had been months on the way, plodding patiently along in the heat and dust, worn and poor, hungry, but supported and sustained by an unwavering faith and belief. It is wonderful, that the power of faith like that can make multitudes upon multitudes of the old and weak and the young and frail enter without hesitation or complaint upon such incredible journeys and endure the resultant miseries without repining."

Jawaharlal Nehru wrote in his book *The Discovery of India*, "In my old city of Allahabad I would attend the great bathing festival, Kumbh Mela, and see hundreds of thousands of people come, as their forebears had come for thousands of years from all over India, to bathe in the Ganges." Mahatma Gandhi mentions the Kumbh Mela in his autobiography: "… and then Kumbh Mela arrived. It was a great moment for me. I have never tried to seek holiness or divinity as a pilgrim, but seventeen lakhs of people cannot be hypocrites."

Investigative research has led to a theory that originally the Kumbh Melas were held only at Haridwar and that the Allahabad Prayagwals or riverside priests consciously created a similar tradition here. They are said to have adapted and grafted epic and puranic scripture onto the local Magh Mela at Allahabad, expanding its scale and authority in response to the politics of colonialism, particularly in its post-Mutiny character. Certain astrological difficulties are also said to exist, complicating the usual assumptions about the Kumbh Mela at Prayag. Xuanzang, medieval Muslim travellers, and British diarists talk of the Magh Mela and the word Kumbh as specially referring to Prayag does not figure before 1870.

The Mela Today

Whatever be the academic debates about the Kumbh, there is no doubt that it means different things to different people. While covering the 2001 Mela for the *Hindustan Times*, I met an illiterate 60-year-old farmer, Chungu, from Ballia (UP), who explained the benefits of a holy dip during the Kumbh. His beliefs were shared by a middle-aged village school teacher from Chandauli (UP), Ram Swaroop, as well as a Gujarati merchant from Rajkot, Chaggan Bhai.

10
Vendor selling the famous guavas of Allahabad at the fair. Courtesy Rajesh Singh.

11
A *mahamandaleshwar* or sect-leader heading across one of the pontoon bridges on his way to the Sangam to perform the *shahi snan* or regal bath as it is traditionally called. Courtesy Rajesh Singh.

Mauni Amavasya, said to be the birth anniversary of the lawgiver Manu, is considered the most important bathing day. The night before, without heeding the chill, millions of people start walking towards the rivers, chanting prayers and mantras. One can occasionally hear chants like "*Har Har Gange!*" piercing the cold winter night.

I saw Sushma Devi, a young mother, dragging her two half-asleep children to the Sangam at 2.30 am. An old couple in their 80s were walking slowly to the river, aided by their sons and grandsons. A poor, childless widow named Suggi, in her 70s, told me that she had saved a fistful of grain from her daily meals, for twelve long years. The small savings that she generated, each day, year after year, helped her attend the fair. She told me that she was not sure of things like salvation and moksha for 88 generations. But it had been her living prayer for 12 years to come to the Kumbh, and she hoped that she would be blessed. People like Suggi challenged my agnosticism.

The recently concluded Ardh Kumbh at Prayag (2007) revolved around the issue of polluted Ganga water. The seers were a divided lot, with some sadhus threatening *jal samadhi* (suicide by drowning in the river) if the Biological Oxygen Demand (BOD) level of the Ganga was not restored. BOD is a measure of the oxygen used by micro-organisms to decompose waste. A smaller number of devotees attended the fair this year, possibly apprehending a terrorist attack, and the pollution of Ganga waters got widespread coverage in the media, though the Mela administration tried to downplay this aspect.

Another interesting feature of the 2007 Mela was the act undertaken by a Japanese woman, Yogmata Kiko Ikoba, for world peace. She stayed in an unventilated underground chamber at the Ardh Kumbh Mela grounds for 72 hours. She entered the nine-foot by nine-foot (c. 3 x 3 metre) chamber on January 18 after rituals and prayers. On completion of *samadhi*, she was conferred the title of "Mahamandaleshwar" by Joona Akhara of the Naga sect.

Referring to his first impressions of the huge crowd, film-maker David Attenborough, whom I interviewed during the Kumbh Mela of 2001, said, "It was frightening to see so many people …. I was amazed that they were so well behaved!"

Journalist Royce Carlson stated, "It is projected that this coming Kumbh Mela (2001) will have between 25 and 30 million people! In order to get an idea of how big this is – the state of California, the most populous state in the U.S., has a population of about 33 million. Imagine fitting almost the entire population of California into just over 50 square kilometres!"

Pamela Constable wrote in the *Washington Post* (January 25, 2001), "The sloping riverside beaches were crammed with more than 25 million pilgrims, a human mass so dense that it simply flowed toward the river and waded as one into the knee-deep water."

12
Sadhus performing rituals in the river. Courtesy Rajesh Singh.

13
Pilgrims taking the holy dip in the icy waters. Courtesy Rajesh Singh.

Laurinda Keys of Associated Press reported (February 21, 2001), "Hundreds of thousands of Hindus took a holy dip in the Ganges river on Wednesday on the last bathing day of the Kumbh Mela, the world's largest religious gathering that organizers said attracted more than 100 million people."

The 2001 Kumbh Mela saw radically changing trends, emblematic of the new millennium. Pamela Constable remarked (*Washington Post*, January 11, 2001), "It's being called Woodstock on the Ganges, the largest public gathering in history, the first experimental nexus between dot-com technology and centuries-old collective ritual." An AFP report on the same day mentioned, "With mobile phone-wielding sadhus, cyber cafes, dedicated websites and satellite TV crews, India's Kumbh Mela – the world's largest religious gathering – has gone high-tech with a vengeance." But despite changes in the Kumbh Mela – seers with laptops and cell phones are now a common sight – its essential spirit continues to draw millions of people from all over the world.

1
A fanciful depiction of Akbar watching over the construction of his Fort at Allahabad, painted by Asit Kumar Haldar (1890–1964). Courtesy Allahabad Museum.

Akbar's Ilahabas

N.R. Farooqi

After the foundation of Turkish rule in India in the early 13th century, the town of Prayag became a part of the Delhi Sultanate but remained in the political wilderness. Kara (65 kilometres northwest of Prayag), however, emerged as a centre of political activity early in the Turkish regime, when it was designated the headquarters of the newly created *iqta* (military/revenue division) of Kara-Manikpur. This town quickly became an alternative site of power in north India and came to be associated with the recalcitrant designs of its governors. It was from Kara that Malik Chajju, nephew of Sultan Balban (r. 1266–86), rebelled against Sultan Jalaluddin Khalji (r. 1290–96). Subsequently, another governor of Kara joined the Sultan's own nephew Ali Gurshasp who staged a successful coup d'etat against his royal uncle, had him assassinated, and usurped the throne of Delhi as Alauddin Khalji (r. 1296–1316). In 1394 when the Sharqi kingdom of Jaunpur was established, Prayag and Kara-Manikpur were seized by the Sharqis. At the turn of the 16th century the Afghans held sway in this region, and it was from the Afghans that Babur, the founder of the Mughal empire in India, captured the town and appointed Sultan Junaid Barlas as its first Mughal governor. The early years of Akbar's reign (1556–1605) saw hectic political activity in this region. Between 1561 and 1574, the emperor was obliged to visit the town four times to keep the eastern provinces of the empire under control.[1]

During his visit to the town in 1574, Akbar seems to have realized its strategic value and decided to make it a military centre. Badauni writes that, in 1574, the Emperor visited Prayag, laid the foundation of a great building, and named the city Ilahabas.[2] Farid Bhakkari and Khafi Khan also mention that in the year 1574 the Emperor arrived at Prayag and laid the foundation of Ilahabad Fort.[3]

Abul Fazl suggests that the Fort and the city of Ilahabas were founded in 1583.[4] But his own testimony that in 1579–80 the town was already known as Ilahabad when it was designated headquarters of the *subah* (province) of the same name, and Badauni's observation that in 1583 when the Emperor went on a pleasure trip to Ilahabad, "which is a new creation on the site of Prayaga", several buildings had already been constructed there,[5] indicate that the foundation stone of the Fort was laid in 1574 and perhaps at that time the town was renamed Ilahabad. Nine years later the Emperor visited the site again; he stayed for four months and began constructing other buildings within the Fort complex under his own supervision.

Mughal chroniclers have designated the city as both Ilahabad and Ilahabas and the contention of some modern scholars that it was Emperor Shahjahan (r. 1627–58) who named it Ilahabad is not true.

2 *above*
Coin struck by Akbar on the founding of Ilahabas. Courtesy Sanjay Garg.

Consequent to its designation as the headquarters of the *subah* of Ilahabad (1580), the town became the residence of the *subahdar* (governor). It was from here that Prince Salim (later Emperor Jahangir) raised the standard of revolt against his father and assumed royal pretensions. It was also from this Fort that the Prince ordered the execution of his father's close confidant, the celebrated historian Abul Fazl whom he regarded his inveterate foe. A Bundela chieftain of the Prince, Bir Singh Deo Bundela, carried out the execution. Abul Fazl's severed head was brought to Allahabad and was probably buried somewhere within the Fort.

During the war of succession between the sons of Shahjahan (1657–59), the city, owing to its strategic location, was coveted by the contestants for the throne. Aurangzeb's triumph over his brother Shah Shuja at Khajwah (near Ilahabad), followed by the capture of Ilahabad Fort, decided the contest in his favour. The city continued to enjoy a great deal of importance even in the 18th century and witnessed, between 1743 and 1751, a prolonged and bloody struggle for its mastery between Ahmad Khan Bangash, Nawab of Farrukhabad, and the ruler of Awadh, Safdar Jung. In 1765, the city had its first glimpse of British paramountcy when the Fort was garrisoned by the British troops as a part of the Treaty of Allahabad. Shortly afterwards the Emperor Shah Alam (r. 1759–1806) arrived in the city to live under British protection. Following the Emperor's later decision to seek Maratha protection and his departure for Delhi (1772), Ilahabad and Kara fell under British control and were sold to Nawab Shuja-ud-daulah, ruler of Awadh, for five million rupees (1773). By the treaty of 1798, Nawab Sadat Ali Khan of Awadh

3
View of the Allahabad Fort. The Fort passed from Mughal into British control on the signing of the historic Treaty of Allahabad on August 9, 1765, between Robert Clive and the Mughal Emperor Shah Alam II. A British garrison was stationed at Allahabad Fort as protection for the insecure Mughal Emperor. Subsequent to Independence the Fort remained in army custody. Efforts are now being made by the army to clear the walls of this heritage structure of the rank vegetation which has sprouted, threatening the structure.

Akbar's Ilahabas

4
The Rani Mahal, the only surviving Mughal structure within the Fort. Also known as the Chalees Sutoon (forty pillars), the edifice was the subject of this aquatint by the British artist, Thomas Daniell. From *Oriental Scenery*, I, no. 6, 1795. Courtesy Victoria Memorial Hall, Kolkata.

was again obliged to surrender Ilahabad Fort along with "all its buildings and appurtenances ... together with as much land surrounding the fort as may be necessary for the purpose of an esplanade" to the British. Three years later, by yet another treaty, the Nawab ceded the entire district of Ilahabad (spelt Allahabad by the British) to the East India Company. This heralded the end of Mughal rule in Allahabad.

Among the Mughal monuments of the city, the most outstanding is the Allahabad Fort. The largest among the forts built by Akbar and situated on the confluence of the rivers Ganga and Yamuna, the Fort served as the symbol of Mughal paramountcy in their eastern territories. Located on the imperial highway and accessible from the capital Agra both by land and by river, the Fort fulfilled, according to Abul Fazl, a long cherished desire of the emperor to build a city and a military centre in this region. Abul Fazl's own testimony that the Emperor intended to use the Fort as a base for punitive expeditions "against the eastern districts and root out the thorns of rebellion from that country"[6] leaves no doubt about the intent of the citadel's use.

According to Abul Fazl, the Emperor had originally planned to construct a complex of four forts but only one was completed in due course. This Fort was divided into four segments. The first contained delightful apartments, situated in the midst of a spacious garden, meant for the residence of the Emperor. The royal seraglio and the residence of the Emperor's distant relatives and personal attendants were situated in the second and third segments respectively, while the fourth housed the barracks for the soldiers.[7] The architect of the Fort is not known but nobles of the stature of Raja Todar Mal, Said Khan, Mukhlis Khan, Rai Bharat Diwan, and Payag Das Munshi were deputed to supervise its construction.[8] The European travellers William Finch and De Laet tell us that nearly 20,000 workers were employed every day for several years for the completion of the project. Along with the fort Akbar also built an embankment 1 *kuroh* (4 kilometres) long, 107 feet (c. 33 metres) broad, and 37 feet (c. 11 metres) tall to protect the city from floods.[9]

The Fort was an irregular triangle enclosed by a high red sandstone wall overshadowed by three imposing gateways, the main one being protected by a deep moat. The Fort is 2,280 yards (2,085 metres) long and 1,560 yards (1,426 metres) broad and covers an area of 983 *bigha*s (about 1.6 square kilometres). According to a 19th-century Indian observer, glass, iron, brick, or other building materials were not used at all in the construction. It was built entirely of stones hewn from rocks on the bank of the river Ganga. A 19th-century document, on the other hand, claims that 33 mansions, three *khwabgah*s (sleeping quarters), 25 gates, 23 bastions, 277 houses, 176 barracks, two audience halls, 77 cellars, one baoli (step-well), five wells, and a canal connecting the Fort with the river Yamuna, were built within the Fort complex.[10]

The interior of the Fort contained numerous elaborate structures but of these the mansion known as the Zenana Mahal or Rani Mahal is the only building of note to have survived in its original shape today. It is a three-storeyed building situated in a spacious courtyard. The ground floor of the building is an extensive hall of 64 pillars while the first floor "bears a large central chamber surrounded by eight ancillary ones and an encompassing veranda".[11]

The famous pillar of the Mauryan Emperor Ashoka is also situated within the Fort complex. Prince Salim is reported to have found it lying on the ground in the Fort when he came to live in Allahabad (1600–04). The pillar was re-erected at his order. The Prince had his complete genealogy inscribed on it below the edicts of Ashoka, Samudragupta, and Raja Birbar. "The names of God," writes a modern scholar, "are interspersed with those of his ancestors, underscoring the Mughal notion that the kings are divinely chosen."[12] During his sojourn in the Fort, Prince Salim also ordered the construction of a black throne for his personal use. The throne was subsequently transferred to Agra Fort in 1611 where it is still preserved. The renowned calligrapher Mir 'Abdullah Katib *mushkin qalam* (musky pen) engraved the name of the Emperor along with the verses praising the throne.

The Fort took several years to complete. According to one estimate, its construction took approximately 45 years, five months, and ten days.[13] In 1611, 37 years after its

5 *above left*
The pillars give the Chalees Sutoon its name, though it actually has 64 pillars.

6
Stone filigree detail and floral motifs in the Chalees Sutoon.

Akbar's Ilahabas

7
The Ashoka pillar which stands within the grounds of Allahabad Fort. Carved on it are the inscriptions of Ashoka, Samudragupta, Raja Birbar, and Jahangir. Among the edicts of Ashoka carved on this pillar, edicts I and II are the most inspirational, affirming the Emperor's reverence for life in all forms, and his love of the sacred law that includes "sinlessness, many good works, compassion, liberality, truthfulness, purity".

8 *opposite*
The tombs of Prince Khusrau (Jahangir's son), his mother Shah Begum, and sister Princess Sultan Nisar Begum. The last tomb is empty as the Princess was eventually buried at Agra. It is said that Khusrau, who was a saintly and popular figure, was buried in remote Allahabad beside the tomb of his mother (Jahangir's first wife) at the prompting of Nur Jahan who was jealous and fearful of the devotion that Khusrau's tomb might attract from the people of Agra.

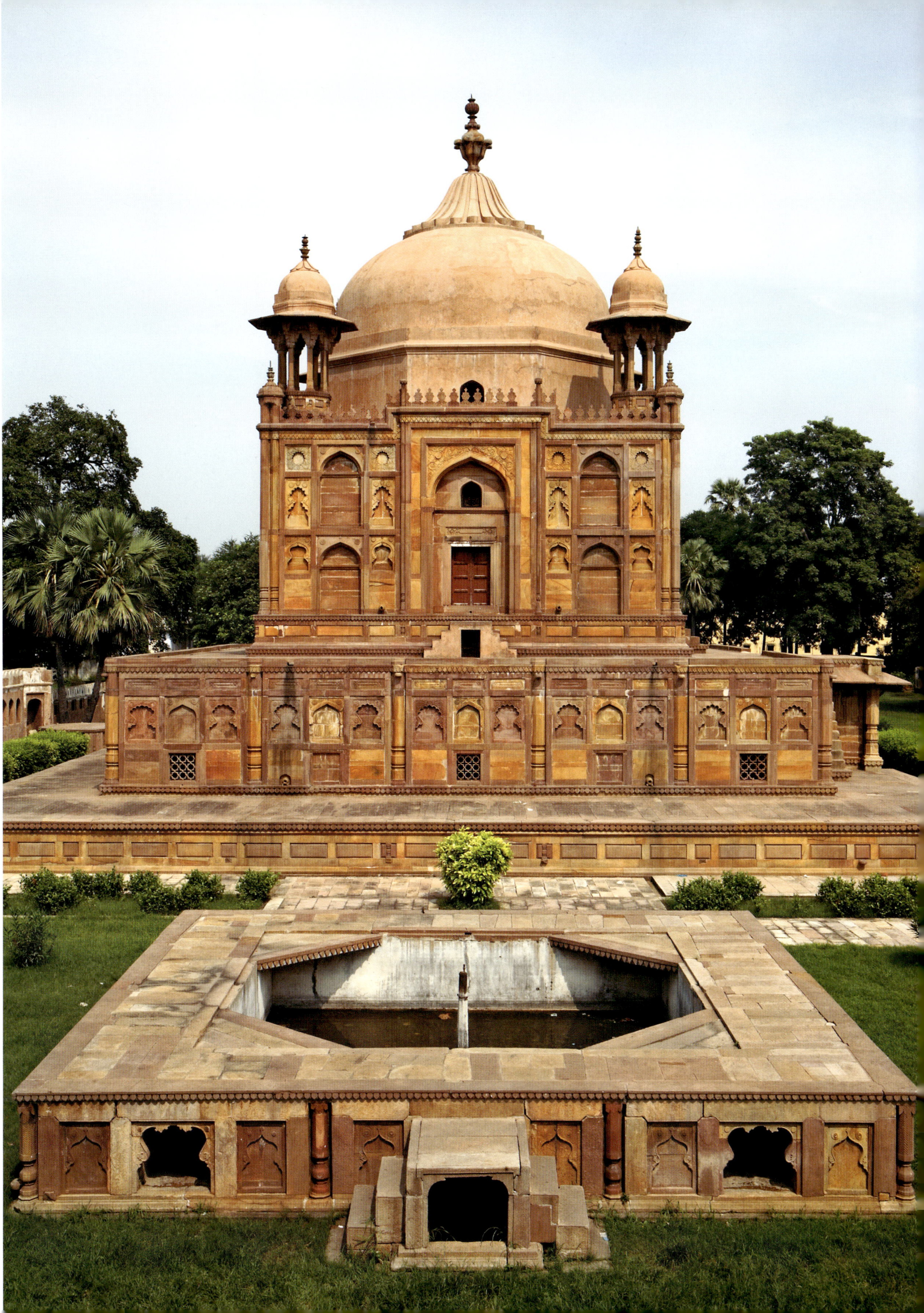

construction began, William Finch found nearly 5,000 workers still working on the project. He wrote that the Fort was far from complete but once completed would turn out to be one of the finest specimens of building art in the world.[14]

The Fort lost much of its originality and architectural beauty when the British occupied it in 1798. Colonel Kyd, the first British commandant of the Fort, started the damage. (The Kydgunj locality of Allahabad was named after him.) The towers and the upper storey of the main gateway were dismantled and a number of batteries and lunettes erected in their place. The battlements on the riverfront were also demolished and the Yamuna gate was closed. The Zenana Mahal was converted into an arsenal and its serene beauty was tarnished by the lime mortar used to cover its walls. Several barracks and residential quarters were also built for British soldiers and officers. Although Lord Curzon later ordered the restoration of the Zenana Mahal to its original state, other buildings of the Fort remained under the control of the ordnance department. The dawn of Independence failed to bring about any change in the Fort's fortune and it continues to hold important establishments of the Ministry of Defence. Consequently, public entry in most parts of the Fort is banned.

During his sojourn in Allahabad, Prince Salim built a *char bagh* (four-part pleasure garden) in the city. Spread over an area of nearly 64 acres and now known as Khusrau Bagh, the garden became the final resting place of Salim's wife and Prince Khusrau's mother Shah Begum (d. 1604). An inscription on the garden's massive western gate gives AH 1014/1606–07 CE as the date of its construction. The tomb itself was probably completed in 1611. It is a three-storeyed structure built entirely of Chunar red sandstone. Mir 'Abdullah Katib *mushkin qalam* engraved the Persian epigraph, giving the date of Shah Begum's death, as well as the inscriptions on the sides

9
View of Khusrau's grave and detail on the vault. Courtesy Rajesh Singh.

10
Interior of Khusrau's burial chamber. Courtesy Rajesh Singh.

of the Begum's cenotaph located on the top floor of the building. Unlike the other royal Mughal tombs, Shah Begum's mausoleum is a relatively simple structure yet its basic plan probably inspired many contemporary architects and "seems to have been a prime source for the design of Akbar's tomb"[15] (at Sikandra, completed by Jahangir after his father's death in 1605). After Khusrau's death (1622), his mortal remains were also interred in the garden and Khusrau's elder sister Princess Sultan Nisar Begum (d. 1646) built a magnificent tomb over his grave. The Princess also constructed a mausoleum for herself in the garden. The last two words of the chronogram on the southern door of the mausoleum (*Rauza-i pak*/chaste tomb) yield AH 1034/1625 CE, which is probably the date of the commencement of its construction. In 1632 when Peter Mundy visited the garden, he found the building still under construction.[16] The Princess was however destined to die in Agra and was buried in her grandfather Akbar's grand mausoleum in nearby Sikandra. This tomb is therefore empty.

The tombs of Khusrau and his sister are double-storeyed and were also built of Chunar sandstone. Their exteriors are practically bereft of any decorative motif but the interiors are embellished with mural paintings of wine vessels, cypresses, geometric designs, and a variety of flowers. The paintings on Sultan Nisar Begum's mausoleum are regarded as "the best preserved examples of painting in any Mughal tomb".[17]

The garden contains a fourth structure as well. Known as Tambolan's Tomb or the House of Tambuli Begum, this structure is as elegant as the other three and was built of Chunar sandstone. The identity of the lady in the tomb is obscure and several anecdotes regarding her place of origin and relationship with the Mughal family are current today. It is however certain that this building was erected later, for in 1632 Peter Mundy[18] refers only to the tombs of Khusrau, his

11
The ornamented walls of Khusrau's burial chamber. Courtesy Rajesh Singh.

mother, and sister and is silent about Tambolan's mausoleum. In the 19th century Tambolan's Tomb was used as the residence of the Garden Superintendent of Allahabad and was restored to its original position after Lord Curzon's visit to Allahabad in 1902.

In Allahabad, Jahangir also built the massive Khuldabad Sarai adjacent to Khusrau Bagh. Bishop Heber, on a visit to the town in 1825, had found the Sarai operational albeit in a dilapidated condition. He calls it "a noble quadrangle, with four fine gothic gateways, surrounded within an embattled wall by a range of cloisters for the accommodation of travellers."[19] Nine years later Bahadur Singh Bhatnagar, the author of *Yadgar-i Bahaduri*, also found the inn intact.[20] Today, apart from its western and eastern gateways, nothing remains of this edifice. Another Mughal monument of Allahabad which no longer exists was the Jami Masjid. Situated on the bank of the Yamuna, where Minto Park now stands, the mosque was built by Shaista Khan in 1645 during his tenure as the *subahdar* of Allahabad. The British demolished the mosque in 1857 in order to punish the city's Muslims for their active role in the Great Uprising. Bishop Heber and subsequently T.W. Beale (1848) both noted the impressive size and architectural beauty of the mosque.[21] The tomb of Zinatunnisa Begum (d. 1761), mother of Mirza Najaf Khan, the Mughal Emperor Shah Alam II's Commander-in-Chief, situated in Begum Bagh (Bahadurgunj) is yet another Mughal monument of the city that has not survived the ravages of time.[22]

Architecture in Mughal India was not only a medium for display of the aesthetic tastes and cultural predilections of its imperial patrons but also served, equally forcefully, to demonstrate their wealth, power, and splendour. Just as centuries ago Ashoka had planted his edicts and pillars in all parts of the subcontinent not only to propagate his teachings but also to create legitimacy for his dynasty, the Mughals deliberately and consciously used their buildings as symbols of their presence and authority in India. In many ways, the buildings left by the Mughals, in Allahabad and elsewhere, continue to serve these objectives even today.

NOTES

1. Abul Fazl, *Akbar Nama*, transl. H. Beveridge, 3 vols., Delhi, 1989 reprint, vol. II, pp. 228–29, 399–401, 428–35; vol. III, p. 124. Abdul Qadir Badauni, *Muntakhab al-Tawarikh*, transl. George Ranking, A.H. Lowe, and W. Haig, 3 vols., Delhi, 1973 reprint, vol. II, pp. 44, 103, 179. Nizamuddin Ahmad, *Tabaqat-i Akbari*, transl. B. De, 3 vols., Delhi, 1992 reprint, vol. II, pp. 256–57, 332–38. Farid Bhakkari, *Zakhirat al-Khawanin*, 3 vols., transl. Z.A. Desai, Delhi, 1993, vol. I, pp. 19–22.
2. Badauni, vol. II, p. 179.
3. Bhakkari, vol. I, p. 108. Muhammad Hashim Khafi Khan, *Muntakhab al-Lubab*, eds. Maulvi Kabiruddin Ahmad and Maulvi Ghulam Qadir, 3 vols., Calcutta, 1860–74, vol. I, p. 236. Ahmad, vol. II, p. 438.
4. Abul Fazl, vol. III, pp. 616–17.
5. Badauni, vol. II, p. 344.
6. Abul Fazl, vol III, p. 616.
7. Ibid., pp. 617–18.
8. T.W. Beale, *Miftah al-Tawarikh*, Agra, 1849, p. 196.
9. Abul Fazl, vol. III, p. 625. Mir Ghulam Husain Tabatabai, *Seir al-Mutakhereen*, 3 vols., Lucknow, 1866, vol. I, p. 190. Irfan Habib, *Atlas of the Mughal Empire*, Oxford University Press, Delhi, 1982, p. 30. Maqbool Ahmad Samdani, *Tarikh-i Ilahabad*, Allahabad, 1938, pp. 293–95. John De Laet, *The Empire of the Great Mogol*, transl. J.S. Hoyland, Delhi, 1974 reprint. William Finch, in Samuel Purchas, *Purchas: His Pilgrims*, Glasgow, 1906, pp. 67–68.
10. Shaligram Srivastava, *Prayag Pradip*, Allahabad, 1937, p. 237.
11. Catherine B. Asher, *Architecture of Mughal India*, Cambridge University Press, Cambridge, 1993, p. 48.
12. Ibid., p. 102.
13. Srivastava, p. 237.
14. See Finch in Purchas, pp. 67–68.
15. Asher, p. 104.
16. Peter Mundy, *Travels of Peter Mundy in India, Europe and Asia (1608–67)*, transl. R.C. Temple, London, 1914.
17. Asher, p. 148.
18. See Mundy.
19. Reginald Heber, *Narratives of a Journey Through the Upper Provinces of India from Calcutta to Bombay*, 3 vols. London, 1828.
20. Bahadur Singh Bhatnagar, *Yadgar-i Bahaduri*.
21. Beale, p. 369.
22. Ibid., p. 518. Samdani, pp. 276–81.

FURTHER READING

Abul Fazl. *Ain-i Akbari*, transl. by H. Blochman, H.S. Jarret, and J.N. Sarkar, Delhi, 1977–78 reprint, 3 vols.

Al-Biruni, Abu Raihan Muhammad Ibn Ahmad. *Kitab al-Hind*, translated by Edward C. Sachau, Delhi, 2003 reprint, 2 vols.

Beni Prasad. *History of Jahangir*, Allahabad, 5th edition, 1973.

Bernier, Francois. *Bernier: Travels in Mughal Empire, 1656–68*, transl. Archibald Constable, revised Vincent A. Smith, Delhi, 1989 reprint.

Beveridge, H. "Sultan Khusrau", *Journal of Royal Asiatic Society of Great Britain and Ireland*, 1907, pp. 597–609.

Fisher, Michael H. (ed.). *First Indian Author of English: Dean Mahomed (1759–1851) in India, Ireland and England*, Oxford University Press, 1996.

Jahangir, Nuruddin Muhammad. *Tuzuk-i Jahangiri*, transl. H. Beveridge and A. Rogers, Delhi, 1968 reprint.

56

Salim's Taswirkhana

Asok Kumar Das

Little did Akbar realize that the formidable red sandstone fort-palace that he built overlooking the confluence of the holy rivers at Allahabad would one day serve as the headquarters of his rebellious son, Prince Salim. For quite some time relations between Salim and his father had been strained. Salim was aware of his father's disapproval of his recent activities and was worried that Akbar might disinherit him and install Salim's son Khusrau as emperor. At this juncture when Akbar commanded Salim to lead the Mewar campaign, the Prince thought it was a ploy to send him off to a distant place, and so he fled to Allahabad in the late summer of 1600. In order to assert his independence he declared himself Shah Salim and started issuing firmans, striking coins, and building up his private entourage.[1] Akbar was unhappy at this turn of events and even planned to travel to Allahabad to chastise Salim, but was prevented from taking any severe action by the senior members of the zenana whom he adored and respected. He chose to wait for the time when good sense would prevail and his only remaining, prodigal son would, on his own, return to the fold.

Allahabad provided an ambience totally different from the pomp and splendour of the imperial courts at Lahore and Agra. Life here revolved around the vast multitude of pilgrims, devotees, and holy men who congregated on the banks of the rivers to take a ritual dip in the confluence on every auspicious day of the Hindu calendar. A curious Salim must have noticed them from the *jharoka* (balcony) of his palace and desired to know more. This is clear from the choice of manuscripts commissioned by him here – *Yoga Vasishtha, Dvadasha Bhava, Raj Kunwar,* and *Bahr al-Hayat* – subjects dealing with Hindu religion and metaphysics, yoga and vedanta. Though Akbar had a deep and abiding interest in different religions and religious texts and had many of them translated into Persian and embellished with appropriate illustrations, Salim had rarely displayed any curiosity before. His brief sojourn at Allahabad provided him the opportunity to interact with yogis and other men of religion and kindled a new desire in his mind to learn about these subjects. Later in life he met the well-known savant, Gosain Jadrup, in Ujjain and Mathura, when he noted in his Memoirs, "He [Jadrup] employs himself in the worship of the true God", and "has thoroughly mastered the sciences of Vedanta, which is the science of Sufism".[2]

Salim had been interested in the arts from an early age. He had built up a collection of manuscripts that included a rare copy of the famous Persian author Arifi's *Guy wa Chawgan,*

1 *opposite*
Prince on Horseback, offering a cup of wine to another prince seated on a tree platform in a hilly landscape. Attributed to Aqa Reza, Allahabad, c. 1600. Detached folio from the Gulshan Album, folio 42.5 x 26.6 cm. Freer Gallery of Art, Washington DC, no. F1954.116b.

given to him by his father "in the polo field in the city of Fatehpur". This was followed by other works like *Risala-yi dar 'Ilm-i Qafia*.[3] He employed a Herati artist, Aqa Reza, sometime before 1586–87, as indicated by an autograph note of Reza's son Abu'l Hasan on an interesting drawing of Saint John executed at Allahabad. We hear more about Salim's growing interest in the arts and his keen desire to collect European pictures – paintings and engravings – and artefacts from the letters and notices of the Jesuits present in Akbar's court at Lahore and Agra. They saw Salim arranging pictures in albums and getting cartoons made from European pictures or instructing his artists to make copies or coloured versions of engravings brought by the Jesuits to the Mughal court that he failed to procure. Many high-quality copies or coloured versions of European pictures of Christian subjects and original engravings from this period have found place in the grand albums that he compiled. Evidence of such work has been found in a minute inscription on a marginal illumination in a folio of the *Muraqqa'-e Gulshan*, in the Gulistan Palace Library, Tehran, written by Aqa Reza "at the Shah Burj in the city of Agra on the twenty-eighth of Ramazan 1008" [April 12, 1600], a few weeks before Salim fled to Allahabad.[4]

Evidently this continued for some time as a number of European engravings carefully coloured by a group of young and old artists, including at least two young women, bearing the legend "Shah Salim" or "Padshah Salim" have been found in the Gulshan *Muraqqa*. Similar paintings signed by painters like Ab'ul Hasan, Mirza Ghulam, Mansur Naqqas, Aqa Reza and others have been traced in other albums – Salim Album, Nasr-al Din Album, and St Petersburg Album – giving an indication of the scale and quality of work commissioned by Salim. Most of these pictures – drawings, tinted drawings, tiny marginal illustrations, and fully coloured paintings (figure 1) – reveal the high quality and craftsmanship demanded by the patron. As many of these are based on Persian masterworks (figure 2) or European engravings and paintings – two principal areas of Salim's interest – it was not surprising that the first three manuscripts commissioned by him in his new art establishment (*taswirkhana*) at Allahabad would include a well-known Persian classic, the *Diwan* of Amir Hasan Dihlawi; a Persian translation of a new work compiled by the Jesuit scholar Father Jeronimo Xavier who was resident at Akbar's court in Agra, *Dastan-e Masih*; and a Hindu metaphysical work, *Yoga Vasishtha*.

The *Diwan*, the first manuscript produced at Allahabad, is an exquisite copy of the collection of *qasida*s, *ghazal*s, *masnawi*s, *ruba'i*s, and *qita*s of the well-known poet Amir Hasan Dihlawi, scribed by the famous Mughal calligrapher Mir 'Abdullah *mushkin qalam* (musky pen) and completed on 27 Muharram 1011 (July 17, 1602), illustrated with 14 superbly finished paintings.[5] The manuscript contains 187 folios and 14 illustrations, mostly full-page, including the interesting picture of Mir 'Abdullah and his assistant under the colophon. (See the previous chapter for more about Mir 'Abdullah's work in Allahabad.)

The paintings of the Amir Hasan manuscript are of high quality, carefully executed on thick, polished paper using a wide range of pigments as noticed in similar works done in the imperial atelier at Agra. Though the name of only one artist has survived, it is possible to recognize the hand of other well known painters who worked for Salim during these rebellious years. It is clear that as many as five of the illustrations were executed by Mirza Ghulam, the stamp of his idiosyncratic style being apparent in some way or the other in all of them. He, like his mentor Aqa Reza, worked exclusively for Salim as revealed by three of his signed works which carry the legend, *murid-e Padshah Salim* (disciple of Padshah Salim). His works here show exceptionally distinctive figure types "with rounded profiles for figures shown in three-quarter view, linear features and extraordinarily long fingers".[6] The landscape with conventional Iranian-type multicolour outcrops or hills and golden sky is typical of his style. The best and the most colourful work of this talented artist in this manuscript is the one showing Suleiman surrounded by winged *peri*s, *jinn*s, a *siagosh* (lynx), a large number of birds including the regulation hoopoe, the mythical *simurgh*, and the poorly attired dervish representing the poet standing before him (figure 3). The stamp of Mirza Ghulam's very characteristic style is apparent everywhere in the miniature – in the bright mustard yellow ground, golden sky, the dresses of the *peri*s and others, and the patterning of the throne. It has a supernatural aura definitely created with a view to emphasize the "Court of Solomon" theme popular in the Persian painting tradition.[7]

On Akbar's suggestion Father Jeronimo Xavier, the Superior of the Third Jesuit Mission to the Mughal court, wrote a book on the life of Christ in Portuguese "that intersperses Gospel stories with Apocrypha and legends from early Church". It was translated into Persian by Abd al-Sattar ibn Qasim Lahori and named *Mirat ul-Quds* (The Mirror of Holiness) or *Dastan-e Masih*. Two copies of the work were prepared at Agra in 1602, one for the Emperor and the other for Prince Salim.[8] Salim, as reported by Xavier, was not satisfied with his copy and "ordered it transcribed in very fine letters on extremely costly paper and ordered paintings made of every scene that possibly could be depicted…. He was not content

2
Court of a Young Prince. Inscribed in the top left-hand corner: "the work of *Reza'i murid-e Padshah Salim*", [Allahabad], c. 1600. Page from the Gulshan Album; 29 x 16.5 cm. Gulistan Palace Library, Tehran.

3
The Poet beseeches Suleiman to grant him a bounty. Attributed to [Mirza] Ghulam, Allahabad, 1602. *Diwan* of Amir Hasan Dihlawi, folio 157a; 20.2 x 10 cm. Walters Art Museum, Baltimore MA, Ms W 650.

Quem penes arbitrium vasti manet æquoris undæ
Per tua, Neptune ô, regna tridente potens
Da facilem ratibusq; viam facilesq; recursus
Hanc Deus humanis adyce rebus opem.

4
Neptune, Lord of the Seas. Coloured copy of a European engraving, [Allahabad], c. 1603. Inscribed in the left- and right-hand sides of the bottom panel: "work of Abu'l Hasan, son of Reza, *murid-e Padshah Salim sannah* 1101 [wrongly written for AH 1011]". 21.5 x 26 cm. Goenka Collection.

with the scenes that had been engraved by Father Nadal,[9] he [Salim] had these painted and many others. It was an extremely lavish book and in Rome one would make great effort to see it."[10]

Recently a *Dastan-e Masih* manuscript of 184 leaves containing 24 miniatures has been found and been attributed to the Allahabad studio of Prince Salim. The manuscript was apparently disturbed with a number of miniatures removed from it.[11] The paintings are superbly finished with a full range of bright colours. The principal characters have been treated with special care. Though the paper used here is thick and of creamish colour, the colouring of the miniatures is generally thin as noticed in most products of the Allahabad studio. Most of the miniatures are stylistically related to those of the *Yoga Vasishtha* and *Raj Kunwar* manuscripts which were taken up by Salim's painters immediately after this manuscript's completion.

Though the artists of Salim's studio made copies of many Christian pictures brought by the Jesuits and produced dozens of drawings and finished pictures of the Virgin, the saints, the nativity, the crucifixion, and apocryphal stories, they produced a distinctly Mughal vision with the figures following Mughal norms. Both Akbar and Salim ordered the artists to visit the Jesuits' chapel and draw copies of whatever they found there and consult these for costume details and colouring. This helped them to illustrate the stories with reasonable accuracy, but the costumes are often of a strange mixed type.

SALIM'S TASWIRKHANA

Some interesting brush drawings and coloured pictures based on European engravings have survived. From the minute signatures on them and the dates given on two of them it is clear that these were prepared for Salim in Allahabad. One of these mentioned earlier is signed by Abu'l Hasan, son of Aqa Reza who has styled himself as a *murid* (devotee) of Padshah Salim, and is dated 1011 (wrongly written as 1101), c. 1603 CE, when they were camping at Allahabad. It shows Neptune, Lord of the Seas, an original engraving on which colours were applied by the painter probably in consultation with the Jesuits (figure 4).[12] Abu'l Hasan uses here the full palette that the Mughal painters employed to make a coloured image out of a monochrome engraving. Several other examples of this type made by celebrated masters of Akbar's *taswirkhana* like Kesavdas, Miskin, and Sanwala have been found.

After Salim's succession as Emperor Jahangir, Abu'l Hasan's rise was meteoric: he attained a very high stature in the *taswirkhana* and was finally awarded the coveted title, *Nadir uz-Zaman*, the Finest in the World, by the Emperor. At least three of his portraits of Jahangir have survived.[13]

Most of the engravings, replicas, and coloured studies of European subjects were mounted in the albums Salim was building up to preserve his ever-increasing collection of Persian, Turkish, early Mughal, and European paintings along with selected passages of calligraphy by great Persian masters. The most celebrated of these albums is the Gulshan Album, the bulk of which is preserved in the Gulistan Palace Library, Tehran. But the prolific output of Salim's artists, old and young, experienced and new, male and female, could not be accommodated in this grand album and smaller albums in a simple format were also commissioned. Devoid of the thick costly papers and extremely lavish gold and coloured embellishments noticed in the Gulshan Album, these are small, simple scrapbooks with a modicum of gold stars and arabesques painted roughly on their narrow margins. However, they house some splendid brush drawings often tinged with colour tones and a limited number of coloured pictures. The best known among these is the Salim Album – now dispersed. Thirty folios from it have been identified in a recent study.[14] In this lot there are seven European subjects including Madonna and Christ Child; five of Hindu, Muslim, and Jain religious men; a portrait of Prince Salim holding a bow and arrow (figure 5); 14 portraits of known and unknown courtiers, scholars, young princes, and a head gardener; two studies of young women; and a solitary landscape scene with a boat. Four of these are inscribed to Basawan, Madhav, Aqa Reza, and (Mirza) Ghulam. The information derived from the signatures or attributions, names of the subjects, and the form of border decoration definitely indicate that the album was made at Allahabad along with older pictures of nobles and holy men in the same collection and later studies of Salim and other unknown young men and women.

The other album made during this period, according to some scholars, consists of pictures showing Salim engaged in shikar and is given the name *Shikarnama*. The six fully painted scenes of the hunt identified as part of this album do not show Salim actually engaged in any specific hunt, but show him in the field examining the kill consisting of rhinos, lions, blackbucks, etc. Salim was fond of hunting and often spent days and weeks in the field, but

5 *opposite*
Prince Salim with Bow and Arrow. Inscribed at top: "This is a portrait of Padshah Salim. May God continue his kingdom forever." Attributed to Abu'l Hasan, Allahabad, c. 1600–04. From the Salim Album, folio 16 x 8.3 cm. Arthur M. Sackler Gallery, Smithsonian Institution, Washington DC, no. S1986.408.

pictures of specific hunting episodes that can be correlated with the text of the *Tuzuk* are rare.[15] These pictures, often pastiches of different shikar scenes, have certain similarities for which they are grouped together. However it is difficult to be sure if they formed part of an album exclusively devoted to Salim's hunting exploits during his stay at Allahabad and earlier.

Jahangir's only reference to manuscript-making in his princely days is found in the *Tuzuk* when he writes about his innovative scheme to have the passages of the *Baburnama* that described birds and animals illustrated with lifelike pictures, and his commissioning of a Persian translation of the Sanskrit *Yogavasishthamaharamayana,* also noted on the opening page of the manuscript of the work written at Allahabad in December 1602. The *Yoga Vasishtha*, as the Persian translation is titled, is a metaphysical text that contains teachings about the illusory nature of material life. In his autograph in the margin of the opening folio Salim writes that the Persian translation was commissioned when he was a prince and declares it as a "good book if one hears it with an ear of intelligence".[16]

There are 41 miniatures in the copy, many full-page, painted in an opulent style incorporating the best achievements of the Mughal studio.[17] These were all originally ascribed, with the names of painters in the margins, but most of these were lost when the manuscript was re-bound. Only seven names survive – Kesav, Khemkaran, Haribans, Bishandas, Hariya, Imam Quli, and Abdul Salim; others were destroyed by the binder's knife. Bishandas stands out for the overall superiority of his style as noticed in his signed work, "The Wise King and the Demon",[18] where the faces are well modelled with expressive eyes, and the colouring is

SALIM'S TASWIRKHANA

چون عفریت از راجه جوابهای عقل پسند موافق نفس الام شنید از سر آزار او درگذشته

اشتهای خود را فراموش کرده در گوشهٔ خلوت رفته بیاد حق مشتغال نمود

muted (figure 6). The figure of the demon that came to devour the king but spared him for his wise replies to his queries is especially noteworthy. At least four other miniatures showing similar expertise in the careful application of muted colours and modelling of faces, and an intimate correlation between the compositional elements, may be attributed to Bishandas.[19] The finest of his works in this manuscript are "King Lavana's Encounter with the Outcaste Women Outside their Hut" and "King Suraghu's Visit to the Hermitage of Sage Mandavya".[20]

The other painter whose style displays the effect of long working experience in Akbar's atelier is Kesav or Kesavdas, a versatile painter who studied European prints, made fully coloured copies of some of them, and borrowed several elements of these in his own works. However, as there was no scope for such variations in this manuscript, no obvious European element is noticeable in the pictures attributable to Kesav here.

The manuscripts produced in the second phase of Salim's stay at Allahabad include *Raj Kunwar*, *Halnama*, and *Dvadasha Bhava*. The first survives in a near complete condition in the Chester Beatty Library, Dublin; the second in the Bibliotheque Nationale, Paris; while the last is fragmented among known and unknown collections abroad. The *Raj Kunwar* manuscript consists of 132 folios illustrated with 51 miniatures. It is a prose romance based on the work of the well-known Jaunpur Sufi poet Qutban, entitled *Mrigavat*. Written in the local Awadhi dialect and completed in 1503, the work is inspired both by Sufi philosophy and folk beliefs based on well-known Hindu elements. The details of how Salim became interested in the story and exactly when he got it translated are not known; however it was likely during his stay at Allahabad as the work enjoyed great popularity there. The present copy was written by the scribe Burhan and completed in 1012 AH (June 1602–May 1604) "in the abode of the sultanate Allahabad".

Raj Kunwar (the prince) became enamoured with the beauty of a doe that was none other than Mrigavat, the Deer Lady. He would not move from the bank of the lotus pond where she had disappeared. His father the king constructed a temple there (figure 7). The prince finally found his beloved but she soon disappeared again to test his true love. While searching for her in the course of a long and perilous journey in the garb of a yogi, the prince met with many supernatural hurdles and challenges before a final happy reunion.

6 *opposite*
The Wise King and the Demon. Signed by Bishandas, Allahabad, 1603. *Yoga Vasishtha*, folio 249a; 28.3 x 17.5 cm. Chester Beatty Library, Dublin, Ms no. 5.

7
Raj Kunwar watches the construction of the temple. Unsigned, Allahabad, 1603. *Raj Kunwar*, folio 9b; 28.3 x 17.5 cm. Chester Beatty Library, Dublin, Ms no. 37.

SALIM'S TASWIRKHANA

8
The Princess, Yogi and the Great Serpent. Unsigned; [Allahabad], c. 1603–04. Dispersed folio from the *Dvadasha Bhava* Ms; 33.2 x 21.5 cm, image: 16.7 x 11.3 cm. Private collection.

The paintings are uneven in quality; some lively and well finished, others lacking in spontaneity. They are very closely related to the illustrations of the *Yoga Vasishtha* completed barely two years earlier, both in size and appearance. Their composition and style also have much in common, giving the impression that the group of painters involved in illustrating the two manuscripts was more or less the same, though not a single name is preserved on the later manuscript. Leach attributed two of the paintings to Kesavdas, three to Bishandas, four to 'Abd al-Salim, three to Salim Quli, and as many as seven to Haribans; the rest to other unspecified painters.[21] On the whole the compositions are uncluttered, containing fewer landscape details or architectural elements than noticeable in other paintings of the imperial *taswirkhana* at Allahabad – even in the Amir Hasan Dihlawi manuscript discussed earlier.

Interestingly, the paintings of this work display figure types, landscape details, and compositions that are in some ways similar to those in a large group of paintings of *Ragamala*, *Rasikapriya*, *Razmnama*, and *Ramayana* prepared for patrons outside the imperial studio from the first decade of the 17th century. Similar stylistic characteristics may also be seen in the *Dvadasha Bhava* produced in Salim's Allahabad studio. An incomplete copy of this unique work, 48 folios with 13 high-quality illustrations, apparently surfaced in a Sotheby's sale in 1972.[22] This is the only existing copy of the Persian translation of the Sanskrit work *Dvadasha Bhava*, "Twelve Existences", originally written for the use of a prince named Mirkanak. The Sanskrit work is now believed to be lost. While there is no inscriptional evidence in the surviving text or copy to associate it with Prince Salim's Allahabad studio, the style and contents of the miniatures are unmistakably similar to the paintings of the Amir Hasan *Diwan*, *Yoga Vasishtha*, and *Raj Kunwar* produced there. The paintings, in the hand of three different painters, often show a teacher and his *chela* (disciple), yogis and other religious men and women, a king, princes, and princesses along with birds, animals, reptiles (figure 8), and sea monsters. A superb example published as frontispiece of the Sotheby's catalogue shows a young prince strewing flowers upon a portrait of a princess in a lovely garden, watched by an old savant in the lower left corner with tiny figures of a teacher and a devotee shown in the distance.

The *Bahr al-Hayat* manuscript in the Chester Beatty Library, a Persian translation of the Sanskrit work *Amrita Kunda*, is also on a subject that would have interested Salim. The copy, consisting of 64 folios and 21 illustrations, deals with the 84 yogic positions to be performed by a *hatha yogi* to attain a state of *samadhi* or final bliss. The only reason why this work is being considered as a product of Salim's Allahabad *taswirkhana* is the close stylistic similarity of the paintings with those of the *Yoga Vasishtha*. There is no colophon to determine the precise year when this was written and illustrated, and none of the pictures bears any name or attribution. They show distinct stylistic traits of four different painters, one amongst them quite accomplished and closest to the *Yoga Vasishtha* miniatures.

The other manuscript prepared for Salim during his stay in Allahabad is a small volume (10.5 x 6.5 cm) of only 31 folios of Arifi's *Halnama*, the Book of Joy, in the Bibliotheque Nationale, first published by Francis Richards.[23] It was calligraphed by the famous scribe "Mir 'Abdullah Katib

9
The opening pages of the *Halnama* of Arifi. Unsigned, copied [at Allahabad] in 1603. Folio size: 10.5 x 6.5 cm, image: 8.5 x 4.2 cm. Bibliotheque Nationale, Paris, Mss Or. Smith-Lesouef 198, folios 1b-2a.

SALIM'S TASWIRKHANA

67

Mushkin Qalam" in the "*kitabkhana* of Sultan Salim at Allahabad in 1012 AH" (1603–04), as mentioned in the colophon. 'Abdullah had completed the volume of Amir Hasan Dihlawi's *Diwan* for Salim only a few months earlier in 1011 AH, and Salim already possessed a manuscript of Arifi's *Guy wa Chawgan* given to him by Akbar, as already noted. The *Halnama* contains only five illustrations, all showing nature in its full glory – gardens, flowers, and flowering trees (figure 9). None of these is signed.

The last manuscript known to have been taken up for illustration in the Allahabad *taswirkhana* deals with the popular subject *Anwar-e Suhayli*, the Persian translation of the well-known Sanskrit work, *Panchatantra*. This was a favourite with Salim's father, who had even commissioned his biographer Abul Fazl to make a new, simpler translation of it. It would be natural for Salim to commission a new manuscript of the *Anwar-e Suhayli* illustrated by his own painters in the "new" style.[24] The work of illustrating the stories was entrusted to Aqa Reza, and he contributed as many as six miniatures, with his son Abu'l Hasan and painters of his circle like Mirza Ghulam and Salim Quli contributing many more. Two pictures in the opening section bear Aqa Reza's signature and appellations *murid-e Padshah Salim* or *be-ikhlas wa murid* and are dated AH 1013 (1604–05). Two others were joint works of Aqa Reza and Muhammad Reza, while two more though not signed by Aqa Reza are in his characteristic style.

Apart from Aqa Reza, Abu'l Hasan, Mirza Ghulam, and Salim Quli, the names of other well known Akbari painters such as Nanha, Dharamdas, Madhav, Anant, Hariya, Durga, Bishandas, Ustad Husain (figure 10), and Rahman Quli are noted in the lower margins of the miniatures. The works of Nanha, Bishandas, Abu'l Hasan, Salim Quli, Dharamdas, and Mirza Ghulam are of particularly fine quality. In fact these signed or attributed works form the basis of identification of many other paintings produced in Salim's Allahabad atelier. The manuscript however remained unfinished and was only completed in 1610–11, as noted in the colophon.

The list may not end here as at least two other manuscripts have inscriptional evidence or stylistic similarity with the manuscripts produced at Allahabad: a well scribed copy of *Nal wa Daman* (Nala-Damayanti) in a private collection with miniatures of very similar style and appearance, including one signed by Salim Quli,[25] and a tiny pocket-size manuscript of *Diwan-e Hafiz* in the British Library

10
The Assembly of the Birds. Ascribed to Ustad Husain, [Allahabad], c. 1604. Folio from *Anwar-e Suhayli*, 12.3 x 7.2 cm. British Library Ms no. Add. 18579, folio 201b.

that bears a fragmentary inscription on the flyleaf recording its possession in Allahabad. Almost all the 19 delicate miniatures of the manuscript have been badly defaced by some orthodox owner at a later stage. Only one bears an attribution to Ustad Madhav written in minute letters on a book held by a person on folio 167a.[26]

After Salim's reconciliation with his father in November 1604 he never returned to Allahabad. The painting atelier must have followed suit. Allahabad prospered as an important outpost of the Mughal empire in the following decades, but never produced any painting or illustrated manuscript after Salim's departure. This brief interregnum in a different set-up at Allahabad must have added a new dimension to his deep interest in collecting and in the arts. Later in his life, as Emperor Jahangir, he had to confront political challenges from his rebellious son Khurram (Shahjahan) and also serious ill-health. His abiding love for the arts and for travel must have helped him to a great extent in facing and overcoming these trials.

NOTES

1 Jalaluddin, "Sultan Salim (Jahangir) as a Rebel King", *Islamic Culture*, April 1973, pp. 121–25. Salim also had a black marble throne made in his name. This is now on view in the Agra Fort where he had it transferred when he became Emperor.

2 A. Rogers and H. Beveridge, *The Tuzuk-i Jahangiri or Memoirs of Jahangir*, Royal Asiatic Society, London, 1909, Vol. 1, pp. 355, 356. For a superb painting illustrating the meeting of Jahangir and Jadrup, now in the Musee Guimet, see Amina Okada, *Indian Miniatures of the Mughal Court*, Harry N. Abrams, New York, 1992, pl. 40.

3 John Seyller, "The Inspection and Valuation of Manuscripts in the Imperial Mughal Library", *Artibus Asiae,* Vol. 57, Nos. 3–4, 1997, pp. 300, 324–25, 335.

4 A.K. Das, "Introduction", in A.K. Das, ed., *Mughal Masters: Further Studies*, Marg Publications, Mumbai, 1998, p. 8, fig. 2.

5 After the initial notice by Richard Ettinghausen (*Paintings of the Sultans and Emperors of India*, New Delhi: Lalit Kala Akademi 1961, pl. 6 and facing text), and subsequent writings by A.K. Das (*Mughal Painting During Jahangir's Time*, Asiatic Society, Calcutta, 1978, pp. 55–60), and Milo C. Beach (*The Grand Mogul*, Williamstown, 1978, pp. 34ff), it was recently published in full by John Seyller ("The Walters Art Museum *Diwan* of Amir Hasan Dihlawi and Salim's Atelier at Allahabad", in Rosemary Crill, Susan Stronge, and Andrew Topsfield, eds., *Arts of Mughal India: Studies in Honour of Robert Skelton*, London: Victoria and Albert Museum, 2004, pp. 95–110). The manuscript is housed in the Walters Art Museum, Baltimore, Md.

6 Seyller, 1997, p. 98.

7 The composition and overall effect of this work can be compared with Mirza Ghulam's signed painting in the British Library *Anwar-e Suhayli*, "The Prince in his Favourite Garden", produced a few years later. J.V.S. Wilkinson, *The Lights of Canopus: Anvar i Suhaili*, The Studio, London, n.d. (1929), pls. vii, ix, xxvii, xxxvi. Other individual studies signed by Ghulam are: (1) "Madonna and Child" in the British Museum: M. Rogers, *Mughal Miniatures*, British Museum Publications, London, 1993, no. 4; (2) "Young Prince" in the Los Angeles County Museum of Art: P. Pal, *Indian Painting, A Catalogue of the Los Angeles Museum of Art*, vol. 1, Los Angeles, 1993, no. 66; (3) "A Prince" in a private collection, sold at Sotheby's London, April 26, 1994, lot 5.

8 The manuscript made for Akbar is damaged but complete, with 11 out of the original 22 illustrations, now in the Lahore Museum, Pakistan. M. Abdullah Chaghtai, "*Mirat al-Quds*, an illustrated manuscript of the Akbar period about

Christ's life", *Lahore Museum Bulletin*, Vol. I, No. 2, 1988, pp. 93–100; Nusrat Ali and Khalid Anis Ahmad, "*Mirat ul-Quds,* The Mirror of Holiness or *Dastan-i Masih,* A Manuscript in Lahore Museum, Pakistan", in Khalid Anis Ansari, ed., *Intercultural Influences in Mughal Painting,* National College of Arts, Lahore, 1995; Gauvin Alexander Bailey, "The Lahore *Mirat al-Quds* and the Impact of Jesuit Theatre on Mughal Painting", *South Asian Studies*, 13, 1997, pp. 31–44.

9   Jerome Nadal, *Adnotationes et Meditations in Evangelia*, Antwerp, 1593.

10   Gauvin Alexander Bailey, *The Jesuits and the Grand Mogul: Renaissance Art at the Imperial Court of India, 1580–1630*, Freer Gallery of Art and Arthur M. Sackler Gallery, Smithsonian Institution, Washington DC, 1998, p. 44, fn. 29, where he quotes from Rome, Archivum Romanum Societatis Iesu, Goa 46l, f. 30b and Goa 14, f. 288a13. I am grateful to Brendan Lynch for supplying full information and a set of photographs of this important document. This has since been acquired by the Cleveland Museum of Art: G.A. Bailey, "Jesuit Art and Architecture in Asia", in John W. O'Malley and G.A. Bailey, eds., *The Jesuits and the Arts 1540–1773*, Saint Joseph's University Press, Philadelphia, 2005, pls. 10.34–10.42.

11   At least one survives in the Fondation Custodia, Paris.

12   C. Singh, "European Themes in Early Mughal Painting", *Chhavi: Golden Jubilee Volume of Bharat Kala Bhavan*, ed. Anand Krishna, Banaras Hindu University, Banaras, 1971, pp. 405–08, pl. 35; B.N. Goswamy and Usha Bhatia, *Painted Visions*, Lalit Kala Akademi, New Delhi, 1999, no. 42. The finest, as also the earliest known work of this talented painter is a delicately drawn little brush drawing of St John, now in the Ashmolean Museum, Oxford. This was based on Albrecht Durer's well-known work "The Crucifixion" (1511). Abu'l Hasan recorded on the drawing that it was executed when he was 13 and that he was a *khanazad*, a term used to denote that he was born when his father was already employed at the court. We notice in this little drawing indication of the Mughal manner of transformation in his treatment suggesting "volume through outline and shaded modeling, skilfully translating the great German engraver's linear hatching into painterly medium of wash". (Andrew Topsfield, *Indian Paintings from Oxford Collections*, Ashmolean Museum in association with the Bodleian Library, Oxford, 1994, pp. 22–23, where he also reproduces the original Durer engraving.)

13   (1) A thumbnail portrait by Daulat, on the margin of a folio of the Gulshan Album in the Gulistan Palace Library, Tehran: Y. Godard, "Les marges du Murakka 'Gulshan'", *Athar-e Iran*, I, 1936, fig.11; (2) "A young painter presenting his work to Shah Salim" in the Bibliotheque Nationale, Paris, Estampes Od 49. 4. no. 40: Okada, 1992, fig. 7; (3) "Young Abul Hasan and others standing before Jahangir" in the British Library (India Office Collection), Johnson Album 27, no. 10: Okada 1992, fig. 4.

14   Elaine Wright, "The Salim Album, c. 1600–1605", in Elaine Wright et al., *Muraqqa': Imperial Mughal Albums from the Chester Beatty Library Dublin*, Art Services International, Alexandra, Va, 2008, pp. 54–67 and pp. 456–58 for a detailed survey and list of earlier notices by S.C. Welch, Milo Beach, Michael Brand and John Lowry, Linda Leach, John Seyller, Joe Dye, etc.

15   The superb picture of the Markhor hunt near Rawalpindi and the incident of hunting a lioness on the bank of the Ana Sagar lake near Ajmer (described in graphic detail in the *Tuzuk* and painted for the *Jahangir Nama)* now preserved in the Maharaja Sawai Man Singh II Museum, City Palace, Jaipur, and in the Indian Museum, Kolkata respectively, are examples of this genre: A.K. Das, *Treasures of Indian Miniatures*, Series One, Maharaja Sawai Man Singh II Museum, Jaipur, 1978, pl. I; A.K. Das, "Mughal Royal Hunt in Miniature Paintings", *Bulletin of the Indian*

Museum, Calcutta, II, 1967, pp. 1–5, pl. 1; and Das, 1978, pp. 151–52.

16   Cf. the translation of the full text made by Seyller: "God is Almighty. I commissioned the translation from Hindi [to Persian] of this book, the *Yoga Vasistha,* one of the stories of the ancients, in the time when I was a prince, at the age of twenty- [paper torn] in the city of [paper torn]. It is a very good book if one hears it with an ear of intelligence. And if one also likes [even] one [story] in a hundred, it is hoped that perhaps [the differences] of its external appearance and internal qualities will be overlooked." John Seyller, "Scribal notes on Mughal manuscript illustrations", *Artibus Asiae*, 1987, p. 300; Wright, 2008, p. 226.

17   For reproductions of some miniatures from this manuscript, see: J. Soustiel and Marie-Christine David, *Miniatures Orientales de l'Inde,* J. Soustiel, Paris, 1973, cover (colour) and pp. 13 (colour), 15; *Indian Miniature Painting from the Collection of Edwin Binney, 3rd,* Portland Art Museum, Portland, 1973, no. 44; Georgina Fantoni, *Indian Painting and Manuscripts,* Sam Fogg, London, 2000, no. 19, etc.

18   Folio 249: Linda Leach, *Mughal and Other Paintings from the Chester Beatty Library*, Scorpion Cavendish, London, 1995, vol. I, pl. 2.31.

19   Ibid., pls. 2.4, 2.14, 2.16, 2.26.

20   Ibid., col. pl. 21; col. pl. 23. See also Wright, 2008, col. pl. 8.

21   Leach, 1995, p. 194.

22   Sotheby's, July 11, 1972, lot 45 (from the Ardeshir Collection).

23   Francis Richards, *A la cour Grand Moghol*, Bibliotheque Nationale and Musee Guimet, Paris, 1986.

24   Fully published by Wilkinson, n.d. (1929), and discussed by Das, 1978, pp. 48–49, 88–94.

25   Muhammad Baqir, "A Rare Moghul Manuscript – Akbar's Copy of Faizi's *Nal wa Daman*", *Pakistan Archaeology*, 8, 1972, pp. 169–72. I am grateful to John Seyller for this reference.

26   The British Library, Grenville XLI, *Diwan-e Hafiz* is discussed by Das, 1978, pp. 83–85; Nora Titley, *Miniatures from Persian Manuscripts; a catalogue and subject index of paintings from Persia, India and Turkey in the British Library and British Museum*, British Library, London, 1977, pp. 58–59; and J. Losty, *Art of the Book in India*, British Library, London, 1982, no. 73.

JOHN HARRISON

For Company and Queen

John Harrison

Allahabad became the capital of a Mughal province in the 1570s and to guard the river crossings at the confluence of the Ganga and Yamuna, Akbar built the last of his magnificent fortress-palaces. The Fort and city came into British hands in 1764 when the East India Company's army defeated the combined forces of the Mughal Emperor and the Nawabs of Awadh and Bengal. Allahabad remained British until 1947, sometimes no more than a district or divisional headquarters, in 1803 briefly capital of a province, in 1833 of a new presidency, but finally from 1858 onwards capital of the United Provinces (UP), until Independence when Lucknow became the capital of the new state of Uttar Pradesh.

The city in the early 19th century was small, half-ruined by warfare, and overshadowed as a port-town by Mirzapur, the centre for cotton, and by Patna, that for opium. But the great Fort retained its strategic importance. Its landward defences were strengthened with European ravelins and bastions: the elegant palace buildings were turned into barracks and the nearby Jama Masjid fitted up "first as a residence for the General ... then used as an assembly room"[1] for social gatherings. Allahabad, the only major UP city with links to Bombay and Nagpur as well as Delhi and Calcutta, became a garrison town, a gunpowder factory, and chief arsenal for the middle Ganga. It was also an administrative centre, its Collector busy seeking to reinvigorate the Mughal land-revenue system, his young deputy, in some stuffy courtroom, hearing legal cases still conducted in Persian – perhaps "drawing a horse or a ship on some blotting paper"[2] to keep himself awake. With police and postal superintendents, a Collector of Customs, the agents for the government's salt and opium monopolies and all their European and Eurasian clerks, together with chaplains and missionaries, a British Allahabad was coming into being. They were housed in a straggle of offices and bungalows along the Yamuna bank between the Fort and Kydgunj and northwards to Colonelgunj and Katra Bazar, though many subordinates lodged in the city and its suburbs.

Of the social life of this European community we have a lively account in the diary of Fanny Parkes, the plump wife of the Collector of Customs. She arrived in 1827, found the Civil Station "pretty and well-ordered; the roads the best in India ..." and made herself at home. She kept cows, goats, rabbits, and turkeys, grew oats for her horses, harvested "marrow-fat peas as fine as in England". She also enjoyed the luxury of numerous servants. Fanny describes her verandah, "... at one end two carpenters are making a wardrobe .... Two silver-smiths are busy making me ornaments after the Hindustanee patterns; the tailors are

1 a and b
The Allahabad Bank building as it looked a quarter century ago (*opposite*). And the building in Chowk which originally housed the bank (*above*). Courtesy John Harrison.

2
The Pioneer Press where Kipling worked from 1887 until 1889. *The Pioneer* was the foremost spokes-paper of British opinion in India and had eminent editors and proprietors like Julian Robinson and George Allen. Rudyard Kipling lived in a bungalow a stone's throw away. Neither the Pioneer Press building nor Kipling's bungalow is standing today. Courtesy John Harrison.

3
Holy Trinity, the oldest church in Allahabad, built in 1839 and modelled on St Martins-in-the-Fields, London. Courtesy John Harrison.

finishing a gown and the *ayah* is polishing silk stockings with a large cowrie shell."³ And while her husband went out shooting or played billiards or squash, she and her friends practised archery, went sketching, or enjoyed a winter gallop round the new racecourse before tea at a table drawn close to the fire.

But then the hot weather arrived, turning Allahabad into Chhota Jahanum, Little Hell. The temperature soared, khas-khas tatties went up at the windows, punkahs swung – in 1832 Fanny even installed a thermantidote, that clumsy manual version of the "desert cooler". The change of season also brought the illness and death under whose shadow everyone lived. In March Fanny's husband succumbed to fever. For 17 days, his head enveloped in bladders of ice, he survived on fresh strawberries and a bottle of claret a day, before recovery began. Five days later Fanny's tailor and under-gardener both died overnight as cholera swept the city.

Allahabad was growing, however. In 1828 Fanny noted, "the first steamer arrived ... from Calcutta, the natives came down in crowds to view it": the city became terminus to a regular service until 1862. In the 1830s the Grand Trunk Road (originally laid by Sher Shah Suri) – that "green-arched, shade-flecked river of life" as Kipling put it – arrived, and 20 years later the railway. A first formal church was built in 1839, Holy Trinity, modelled on St Martins-in-the-Fields in London. Baptist missionaries appeared, closely followed by American Presbyterians who brought a printing press, soon busy with tracts and translations in Arabic, Hindi, and Roman-Urdu. They preached in the Chowk, winning few converts, but the High School they opened near the Yamuna had attracted 550 pupils by 1855. There was also a blind and leper asylum, an orphanage, and a Poor House for the destitute elderly. Society undertook good works, too.

Then in 1857 the East India Company's authority was swept away across all north India. At Allahabad the barracks, bungalows, and new railway station were all looted or burned; only the Fort held out until troops arrived to relieve it. It was thus at Allahabad that Governor General Canning directed the re-conquest of northern India and the pacification of Awadh, and on the first of November 1858 read out Queen Victoria's proclamation taking India under the Crown and her promise of clemency, religious neutrality, and the equal and impartial protection of the law. On land confiscated for rebellion a new European Allahabad would now be spaciously laid out.

The tracks, marshalling yards, and fenced quarters of the East India Railway formed a defensive barrier, with just two road-links to the Indian city, now seen as potentially dangerous. Manning it were the drivers, firemen, fitters and boiler inspectors, signalmen and station staff, all British or Anglo-Indian. They formed a self-conscious closed community, with their own cooperative society, radical newspaper, schools, hospitals, club, and sports-grounds – even their own chaplain who for a while took services in a disused rum godown.

4
All Saints Cathedral, constructed by Frizzoni & Co. to the design of Sir William Emerson, was originally intended for an Australian city but found itself in Allahabad. Courtesy Rajesh Singh.

FOR COMPANY AND QUEEN

5
A historic church near the Kotwali in Chowk.

Behind them stood the regular police force, European and Anglo-Indian down to sergeant level, with their own Lines off Stanley Road. They were the active day-to-day manifestation of imperial power ready to restore order in a city riot or control the multitude of pilgrims at the Magh Mela.

Finally, in a great arc of artillery, cavalry, and infantry lines, came the army, force held in reserve. The troops which manned this perimeter were still both Indian and British but the number of Europeans was doubled post-Mutiny and the artillery put entirely in their hands. It was a world of parade grounds, rifle butts, and barracks built – on Florence Nightingale's insistence – like vast airy barns, 200 by 100 feet (72 x 36 m) with ceilings 40 feet (c. 15 m) high. Here the men lined out their beds and the regulation kit boxes in which all their possessions were kept. This was the soldier's Allahabad, his universe for a five- to seven-year tour of duty.

He escaped these bounds only on route marches, field exercises, and church parades, or an occasional flag march through the city in a show of force. Otherwise there was only the interminable round of drill, parades, sentry-duty, and kit inspections. The hot weather brought prickly heat and a sweaty idleness – and a great part of the time the British soldier slept, principally because he had nothing else to do. No wonder tempers frayed and on pay-day there was so much boozing in the canteen and so many lining up for a visit to the

6
The bungalow of the Garden-in-Charge of the Company Bagh, as it was popularly called. Laid out on the site of villages destroyed by Neill's forces after the uprising of 1857, the Company Bagh was officially christened Alfred Park (after Prince Alfred, Duke of Edinburgh, who visited the city) and is now called Chandra Shekhar Azad Park. The extensive gardens held the Thornhill-Mayne Library and the Gymkhana Club. They now encompass the Allahabad Museum, the Azad monument, the local stadium, the Prayag Sangeet Samiti, the Hindustani Academy, and the Ganganatha Jha Research Institute for Sanskrit Studies.

FOR COMPANY AND QUEEN

7
The Palace Theatre in the Civil Lines, the auditorium and cinema-hall once reserved for Europeans. A favourite with local viewers with cosmopolitan tastes well into the 1970s, it was a popular venue for Sunday matinee enthusiasts. It closed down in 2009.

regimental brothel. The women were medically inspected, but till the First World War 25 per cent or more of British troops were disabled by venereal disease. Thereafter things improved as "dry" canteens appeared, along with more games and reading rooms, and Macpherson Lake was opened for bathing.

It was within these encircling defences that the Civil Lines were built. First came South Road, parallel to the railway, some 40 three-acre plots for hotels and "shops for the sale of Europe goods". This was followed by the main east–west artery, Canning Road (now Mahatma Gandhi Marg) with further shops and offices, each in its large compound. The vertical axis, Queen's Road, running north from the station, was lined with public buildings: a railway hospital, telegraph office, Laurie's Hotel (now the Municipality), the Anglican Cathedral in rose and cream on an island site, and then the Government Press, the Accountant-General's warren of offices, and the four severely handsome blocks housing the High Court and Secretariat. On these two axes further parallel roads were built, carving out three-acre plots for four bungalows apiece with servants' quarters at the rear. The earliest bungalows were often of sun-dried brick, with a roof of country tiles sweeping down to the edge of the verandah. Later, plinths and door- and window-surrounds were more usually of fired brick, with a split roof of Frizzoni tiles and clerestory windows. Heat not cold being the problem, outer rooms opened straight on to the verandah and were all interconnected. Privacy was provided by the sheer size of the compound.

Few officials stayed long enough in one posting to build for themselves, so speculative builders stepped in – coach-

John Harrison

builder Thomas Wharton, the railway-contractor Robert Carr, the Armenian, Elias, whose bungalow Blanche Villa was built for £400, let for £145 a year, and sold in 1872 for £1,500. Two more considerable firms would join them: Frizzoni & Co. and Vassal & Co., Italian and German respectively. They employed architects and some 1,200 workmen between them. It was they who built St Mary's Convent, the Italianate Roman Catholic cathedral, the Allahabad flour-mills, Ewing Christian College, and the ballroom of the Allahabad Club.

Such firms raised capital from four private banks in Allahabad, all under British management. The Allahabad Bank flourished, moving from its city base to lush gardens off Cawnpore Road where a huge mosquito-proof cage in the middle of the lawn enabled the manager to entertain guests and sleep in comfort in the open air. These banks also financed cinemas, printing presses, and the engineering works of Thomas Crawley. He it was with his huge ice machines who contracted to supply ice, at any hour, day or night, from April to October, and who built the railings and bandstand in Alfred Park and the iron "filth carts" in which the night-soil of the Civil Lines was trundled out of town. The collateral such firms offered – the steam hammers and drills of Crawley or the tins of oysters and truffles, the quarts of champagne, claret, and hock at Laurie's Hotel, are recorded in the Sub-Registrar's volumes.

Since there were many bachelors, grass-widowers, and clerks on modest pay, bungalows were often shared. In 1904, No. 25 Cawnpore Road was split into five parts at Rs 28 per month apiece. Often too servants' quarters were let out – to 15 tenants in one case, 35 in another. Large compounds might be splendid with flowers, vegetables, and orchards – or unsanitary standing ground for milch cattle and tonga ponies.

8 *opposite*
A cinema-bill dating back to 1937. Courtesy Neelum Saran Gour.

9
The bungalow housing the Cosmopolitan Club, formerly the European Club, which was closed to Anglo-Indians and Indians alike. This was the site where Nityanand Chatterjee, disguised as a waiter, hurled a bomb at the British Governor.

For Company and Queen

10
This empty marble pedestal in the former Alfred Park once held an imposing statue of Queen Victoria.

11 *opposite*
The Minto Park Monument with Queen Victoria's proclamation of November 1, 1857, which was read out by Lord Canning and marked the closure of the East India Company and the takeover of the subcontinent by the British Crown.

Making Allahabad a provincial capital drew to it not only a Lieutenant-Governor and his entourage but the full range of departments: Forests, for example, the PWD, and the Government Press with its 1,000 employees – before the typewriter all official correspondence was printed! The installation of the High Court in 1869 and the transformation of Muir College into a University in 1887 brought yet more Europeans to Allahabad.

To minister to this flock more churches were built – including the Scotch Kirk, St Patrick's, and the Anglican and Roman Catholic Cathedrals. Missionaries also supported education, the Anglican Girls and Boys High Schools being matched by Catholic St Mary's Free School and St Joseph's Collegiate, with Ewing Christian College, Holland Hall, and the very practical Agricultural Institute at Naini as the American Presbyterians' contribution. The Christian Tract and Book Society and the imposing Bible House testify to their vast output in print. They also created dispensaries, clinics, and hospitals such as the Sara Seward Memorial Hospital with its emphasis on women's needs and associated training school for nurses.

Allahabad was also home to the *Hindustan Review* of the Kayastha community. *The Pioneer*, for which Kipling worked, provided a powerful voice for European views and interests; *The Leader* spoke for nationalist Indians. The University itself took a remarkable range of international journals.

As railways spread and in 1869 the Suez Canal was completed, another change took place. It became easier for officers and civilians to marry. Medical advances made India safer and the Indian services were well-paid and pensioned. So, more young wives came out to the Allahabad world of bungalows, gardens, and servants. Even the hot weather lost its terrors as escape to the hills became possible.

However, there were few active roles for European women in India beyond organizing a temporary home and bringing up children. Teaching in girls' schools, clerical work, a nursing or hospital career

For Company and Queen

were all low-status jobs for single women. Some wives did join their husbands on tour, but the tennis party or picnic were more usual, perhaps with service on a charity committee. Official hierarchy limited the group a wife mixed with, dictating where she sat at table and with whom therefore she talked about promotions and transfers, prices and servants, club gossip – and the failings of Indians. For many women India was an exile – emphatically so for those whose children had been sent home to school.

A newcomer might rent his house furnished or unfurnished – from the builder perhaps or one of the great Indian merchant-bankers like Bachchaji from Rani Mandi who had gone into property. New furniture could be had from Luscombe's factory, a piano from Harry Clarke, while L. de Souza conducted regular auctions: Miss Mutlow's furniture, the splendid collection of plants of Dr Glynn-Griffiths, or a landau, harness, and handsome grey walers, "the property of G.W. Allen, CIE, gone home". For day-to-day shopping Europeans turned to Katra with its Indian fruit, vegetable, grain, and cloth merchants whose shops then had open fields behind them, or sent their servants to the municipal covered market for meat and fish, or visited the European shops on Canning Road. Here were branches of such famous Calcutta department stores as Whiteway and Laidlaw, staffed with English girls to set an exclusive tone, or the less intimidating Hathaway's. Alongside were Wheeler's booksellers and stationers, Kellner's with their own pig and dairy farm in the Hills, Dagg the German jeweller-photographer, Cline & Co. "dressmakers and milliners, est^d 1888", gunsmiths, a saddler, and at No. 14 Buncombe's whose palatial bungalow amongst spacious lawns was both a pharmacy and pastrycook's. (Transformed from Buncombe's into Barnett's Hotel it remained "The House of Fresh Confectionery", provider of refreshments for Allahabad's annual polo week.) In 1922 M.J. Arratoon offered first-class cars on hire at Rs 6 per hour and the provision merchant R.M. Guzder ran a petrol pump on Albert Road. As the Automobile Association's 1929 *AA Book of the Road* records, Allahabad had hotels for Europeans, Anglo-Indians, Hindus, and Muslims and equally separate clubs – the Allahabad Club for Europeans, the United for both Europeans and Anglo-Indians, and the Thornhill for Anglo-Indians only.

Class and race shaped the physical and mental map of the Civil Lines. A prescribed minimum value was laid down for every bungalow built. Housing a much-needed electricity foreman – a poor European – on Hastings Road was a dreadful problem until a low-lying, ravined half-plot "not suitable for a Government Official or Better Class European", was found. Anglo-Indians were generally excluded, their small Thornhill settlement pushed to the fringe of the Civil Lines. At the 1921 Census while only 87 Europeans were recorded as living in the city, 1,548 Anglo-Indians did so. The Indian Christian employees of the Government Press, moved from Agra to Allahabad post-Mutiny, were housed well outside the Civil Lines at Muirabad. Indians were at first excluded – except for the seemingly invisible army of servants.

But as early as 1893 P.C. Banerji was a High Court judge and in the 20th century, on the civil side, the legal profession was dominated by men like Motilal Nehru, Tej Bahadur Sapru who would become Law Member in the Government of India, and Sunder Lal Dave, Vice-Chancellor of two universities. But for his untimely death,

12
The Thornhill-Mayne Library, now known as the Public Library. Built in 1878, it is named after two civil servants, Francis Otway Mayne and Cadwent Bensley Thornhill.

Allahabad would also have had an Indian Christian, S.K. Rudra, as Vice-Chancellor. Many of his Indian professorial colleagues were armed with higher degrees from England and America. Such men could not be, and were not, long excluded.

Moreover, institutions like the Municipality increasingly embraced both Civil Lines and City. As Allahabad grew, it had to take over services once left to private hands. Open public tanks or household wells – in the city often sunk close to the dry well or *sandak* used as latrine – invited epidemic disease. The remedy lay in a municipal waterworks supplying standpipes and pipelines for everyone, followed by drainage schemes to carry off the water. With paraffin came municipal street lighting and from 1912 electricity, eagerly taken up by traders whether on Canning Road or in the Chowk. Corporate planning went further with the establishment in 1919 of an Improvement Trust, which drove new roads through congested *mohulla*s to introduce fresh air – and traffic – and created new planned neighbourhoods, with in-built open space, at George Town and Alopi Bagh, Katra and Mumfordgunj.

Organizing these amenities and securing taxes to pay for them required a measure of popular consent. From 1868 the Municipality became an elective body, with representatives from both City and Civil Lines wards. The whole cooperative apparatus of committees, agendas, and minutes appeared, with a *Municipal Gazette* under Jawaharlal Nehru's chairmanship to publicize proceedings. Political change proceeded locally as well as nationally.

On every sort of committee – hospital, school, library, Bar Association, or University Senate – Europeans and Indians increasingly shared power and responsibility. They joined forces in sport, they shared rivalries at the Alfred Park flower-show. As the proportion of Indian children allowed at grant-aided European schools rose from 15 to 25 per cent, more Indian parents attended both sports-days and speech-days or helped with Scouts and Girl Guides. The membership of Allahabad's two Masonic Lodges was as mixed and varied as that of the Automobile Association which welcomed both the

13
Entrance gallery and porch of the Public Library.

Chief Justice Sir Grimwood Mears, and the Municipal Engineer Mr M.C. Gupta.

Of this Civil Station, this European world, what may survive? Not the modest bungalows in spacious compounds, now being demolished and built over. The roads with their trees, stunted by age and goatherds, may remain, but the early-morning canter has been replaced by the thunder of lorries. The Allahabad Club has gone, kites are flown from the polo ground – but cricket and football flourish. While chapels, churches, and the two cathedrals empty, the High Court and the University overflow. The public buildings whose spires and towers call to one another across the Civil Lines – Holy Trinity to Senate House; Vizianagram Hall to Public Library; the bizarre Mayo Hall to the two cathedrals – seem likely to survive; the railways and their great bridges certainly will, memorials of a vanished British Allahabad.

But British Allahabad was not just a matter of buildings and institutions, it was one of ideas and attitudes too, from which Indians could choose as they wished: the English language, its prose, the novel and short story, and Western science and technology; bureaucracy but democracy too; a concern with the public good – a corporate provision of schools, hospitals, water, and sanitation; the rights of the individual, woman and man; officialdom's accountability to independent secular courts. Which of these will survive only time will tell.

NOTES

1   Reginald B. Heber, *Narratives of a Journey Through the Upper Provinces of India from Calcutta to Bombay*, 3 vols., London, 1828, vol. I, p. 333.
2   James Wilson in a letter to John Bight, London, 1854.
3   Fanny Parkes, *Wanderings of a Pilgrim in Search of the Picturesque, during Four-and-twenty Years in the East, with Revelations of Life in the Zenana*, London, 1850.

14
Details on the carved pillars of the entrance gallery of the Public Library, depicting native craftsmen at work.

भारत सरकार एवं यू.एन.डी.पी. के सहयोग से, क्षेत्रीय नगर पर्यावरण केन्द्र लखनऊ के निर्देशन में
उ.प्र. इलेक्ट्रानिक्स कारपोरेशन लि. व नगर निगम इलाहाबाद द्वारा
सम्पत्ती कर सुधार एवं क्षमता विकास कार्यक्रम में अभिवृद्धि हेतु
नगर को स्वच्छ बनाना है
नई रोशनी लाना है
ग्रोसरी

Vande Bharatam

Badri Narayan Tiwari and Neelum Saran Gour

If a specific point of commencement to the Indian National Movement is sought, historians' choice would fall on 1857.

The Uprising
News of the Uprising at Meerut and Delhi arrived in Allahabad on May 12. The city was then held by the 6th Native Infantry – 200 Sikhs and 107 British officers. Under an assurance of loyalty given by the local sepoys, a number of British families who had earlier rushed to seek sanctuary in the Fort returned to their bungalows. However as reports of military uprisings in regions very close to Allahabad, such as Banaras and Pratapgarh, started pouring into the city, British officers became uneasy about the reliability of the promise made by the Indian sepoys. On May 19 some senior British civilian officers were called in from Pratapgarh to protect the treasury and the jail. It was resolved to shift the treasury, which contained nearly Rs 30 lakhs, to the Fort, for which vehicles were required, but the plan was abandoned because it was felt that it would not be prudent to entrust such a large amount to the Indian sepoys. Additionally, it was felt that the Sikh soldiers in the Fort might be tempted at the sight of the money and rise in revolt too. On June 6, as panic grew, the British officers decided to disarm the Indian sepoys. The sepoys, for their part, got together and resolved not to obey orders. Carrying their arms they headed for the army camp in Alopi Bagh where the 6th regiment was posted. When they reached the camp, the captain, without considering that both sides were Indian, ordered his regiment to be ready with their guns. The regiment obeyed, and opened fire, but no one was hurt because the guns were fired in the air and not aimed at the soldiers on the opposite side. This incident marked the start of the rebellion in Allahabad. All the regiments posted in the city, cavalry and infantry, came together and took to the streets, shooting down British residents in the city, especially army officers. Many innocent British people lost their lives in the firings.

1 *opposite*
The neem tree near the Kotwali which served as the gallows for hanging hundreds of rebels after the Uprising.

2 *above*
Neill's forces took the city by storm on June 11, 1857, and a reign of terror ensued. Engraving from a book. Courtesy Allahabad Museum.

3
A tea vendor now plies his trade beneath the historic neem.

Firing indiscriminately at all the British in sight, the Indian sepoys reached the parade ground. By then it was nine at night, an hour when most British officers were at home. Many of them were unaware of the storm brewing in the city. The Indian sepoys burst a cracker in the air to announce the beginning of the Revolt, which was heard by the British officers living nearby. They immediately rushed to the parade ground, some struggling into their uniforms and some in plain clothes. Most were quite sure of their ability to quell the rebellious soldiers but the situation was clearly beyond control and every British officer was shot down. Some like Lieutenant Hicks managed to escape to the Fort across the Ganga. Others like Lieutenant Harvard and Lieutenant Alexander reached the parade ground only to be killed.

In the Allahabad Cantonment, which at that time was in the Chatham Lines to the north of Colonelgunj, a bugle signalling the beginning of the Revolt was blown at the same time, and was heard by the officers living in the Cantonment. They too rushed to the Cantonment but were shot down, all except three who somehow managed to escape with their lives. The view from the Fort is described in a letter written by Charles Chester, the Commissioner:

> Shortly after ten p.m. fires began to be visible … until the horizon looking North from the ramparts of the fort was one inchasing map of flame and horrid smoke, from which opened the firearms and yells of thousands of infuriated devils doing the work of murder and rapine. (Letter to George Frederick Edmonstone, Lieutenant Governor of the North-West Provinces from 1859 to 1863.)

The situation was confounded by the fact that abundant liquor stocks were freely plundered by both Europeans and Sikhs, with the result that "a reign of intoxication had commenced, which subverted all military authority, leaving the garrison in a condition of shameful helplessness" (Colonel Neill's version).

Initially operating from Alopi Bagh, the rebels occupied Daragunj and the bridge of boats. Railways were damaged, telegraph wires cut, jails broken open, and wild plunder prevailed everywhere. After killing the Europeans and burning their bungalows and looting their property, popular wrath turned on the local Bengalis who were looked upon as sycophants of the British. Inside the Fort a crowd of hounded European families huddled together in sickness and terror while Captains Brasyer and Hastewood and Lieutenants Rupett and Brown somehow held the Fort. The rebels looted the treasury containing Rs 30 lakhs. Earlier the intention had been to take the money to Delhi and hand it to Bahadur Shah Zafar, the disempowered Mughal Emperor, but later the soldiers decided to divide the money amongst themselves instead. More soldiers were told to help themselves to the money in other treasuries under the control of the British in the city. In a short while all the treasuries in Allahabad were looted and the money divided among the Indian sepoys.

Liaqat Ali: At this point a *maulvi* named Liaqat Ali, who lived in a mosque in the Cantonment, hung up a green flag outside the mosque and declared it to be his sultanate with himself as the governor representing the Mughal Emperor. He then addressed a large gathering made up of villagers and rebels and released criminals and exhorted them to form an army and prepare for a holy crusade or *jehad*, as he called it. Allahabad and its adjoining regions beginning with the Khusrau Bagh, became Liaqat Ali's sultanate. His private army planned to capture the Fort but was thwarted on June 11 by Colonel Neill's arrival. Liaqat Ali escaped to Kanpur with a price on his head and was captured in Bombay only in 1871. At his trial he was asked to apologize, in which case he could be let off as a respected Muslim cleric. But Liaqat Ali's answer to his English judge was that he feared neither imprisonment nor hanging and preferred death to lying. He

4
The solitary grave of a young English soldier in Company Bagh, now an object of veneration for the park's *mali*s or gardeners by whom the grave is devotedly maintained. Incense is lit and an entire mythology has been built around the persona of the wish-fulfilling "Richard Sahib", as he is fondly called. (His name was not Richard, incidentally.) By the accounts of the *mali*s of Alfred Park, Richard Sahib is often sighted wearing his red coat and white breeches and carrying a musket. He is partial to offerings of liquor and cigarettes. He also turns himself into a duck when he pleases. Postcolonial fantasy has exercised itself to the farthest reaches of imagination here.

declared that he had spared no occasion to provoke rebellion nor let pass any opportunity to kill Europeans, though he claimed to have also rescued innocent British women and children, like the family of a certain Mrs Bennet, when the occasion demanded. He was sentenced to life imprisonment in the Andamans.

Sangram Singh: Defeated by Neill's forces, the fleeing rebels ran towards the Phaphamau Bridge across the Ganga. As these soldiers possessed a part of the money looted from the treasury, they decided to go to a small village called Shahabpur some distance from the city and hand over the money for safe keeping to the zamindar of the village, Sangram Singh, who was sympathetic towards the rebel cause. Sangram Singh accepted the money and gave them a receipt for it. In addition he gave the rebel Mewatis shelter in his village and employment as servants in his bungalow. When Captain Chapman, a British army officer who had been given the responsibility of suppressing the Revolt in that region, heard of this, he ordered his soldiers to

5
Graves of British soldiers who fell during the 1857 Uprising, at the Kydgunj cemetery near the Fort.

surround the bungalow. The Pasis, who lived around the boundary of Sangram Singh's bungalow and worked as his security guards, retaliated against the British soldiers with knives, sticks, and spears. Although they were no match for the soldiers, who were armed with sophisticated weapons, they held their ground for two days. At the end of two days the soldiers managed to reach the bungalow but Sangram Singh's guards began burning red chilli powder inside the bungalow, which sent the British soldiers running helter skelter. In the meantime Sangram Singh, who was himself a valiant fighter, decided to join the battle against the British. A large number of villagers, too, decided to go to the nearby forest of Panchdevra to mount the fight from there. In the forest was a famous temple to Goddess Kali, which Sangram Singh himself had constructed. The temple became the headquarters of Sangram Singh's army. The battle ended on the eighteenth day when Captain Chapman chopped off Sangram Singh's head. Since Sangram Singh was a large man his head was likewise massive. When Captain Chapman presented the head to the British judge who had been appointed by the government to pass instant judgement against the Indian rebels, the judge rebuked him, saying that such a brave man should have been caught alive and not killed so mercilessly. Sangram Singh's head was later handed over to the villagers of Shahabpur, who buried it under a mango tree in an orchard and built a mound over it to mark the spot.

Even 150 years after the Rebellion, Sangram Singh still holds a special place in the oral narratives of the villagers of Shahabpur. It is part of the oral history of the village that on one occasion Sangram Singh appeared in the dreams of some of the villagers and assured them that he was protecting the village. Since then Sangram Singh has become a deity of the village and the mound has become a sacred place. So runs the narrative of the village.

As a reward for killing Sangram Singh and controlling the Revolt, Captain Chapman was conferred the entire village and was also given Sangram Singh's bungalow to live in. The first thing he did

6
Chandra Shekhar Azad's statue, erected at the spot of his martyrdom in a police ambush in February 1931. The park currently bears his name.

Vande Bharatam 91

7
Photograph following Azad's killing and the pistol taken from him as a trophy by the police officer John Knot Bower. Courtesy Allahabad Museum.

8
Swaraj Bhavan, the home of Motilal Nehru, and the scene of much nationalist agitation. Originally called Mahmud Manzil, it had belonged to Sir Syed Ahmad Khan, whose son Syed Mahmud was the first Indian judge at the Allahabad High Court. Subsequently bought by Motilal Nehru, it turned into a vibrant centre for anti-British activity. The vast lawns were the scene of the famous Holi bonfire of 1920 which Motilal Nehru organized, in which piles of foreign clothes were set alight in symbolic pledge to the Swadeshi principle. Now a heritage museum, it was the headquarters of the All India Congress Committee until 1946.

was banish the Pasis comprising Sangram Singh's security guards to the outskirts of the village, where they live even today. He demolished the bungalow and built a new one, which still stands. Since the new bungalow was built over the plinth of the earlier one, it is on a high elevation. Captain Chapman lived in the bungalow for many years with his wife. He later sold it to the Raja of Pratapgarh whose descendants now live in it.

The Reckoning: To return to the city of Allahabad proper, when Colonel Neill and later General Havelock appeared on the scene, a chapter of reverse atrocities ensued. Between June 12 and 19, the British retook the city and an intensive and brutal vengeance began. Entire villages were laid waste, suburbs set afire, hundreds of men hanged, hundreds of women drowned in wells into which they had jumped to escape dishonour. British retribution was rigorous.

"We have the power of life in our hands and I assure you, we spare not. The condemned culprit is placed under a tree with a rope round his neck on the top of

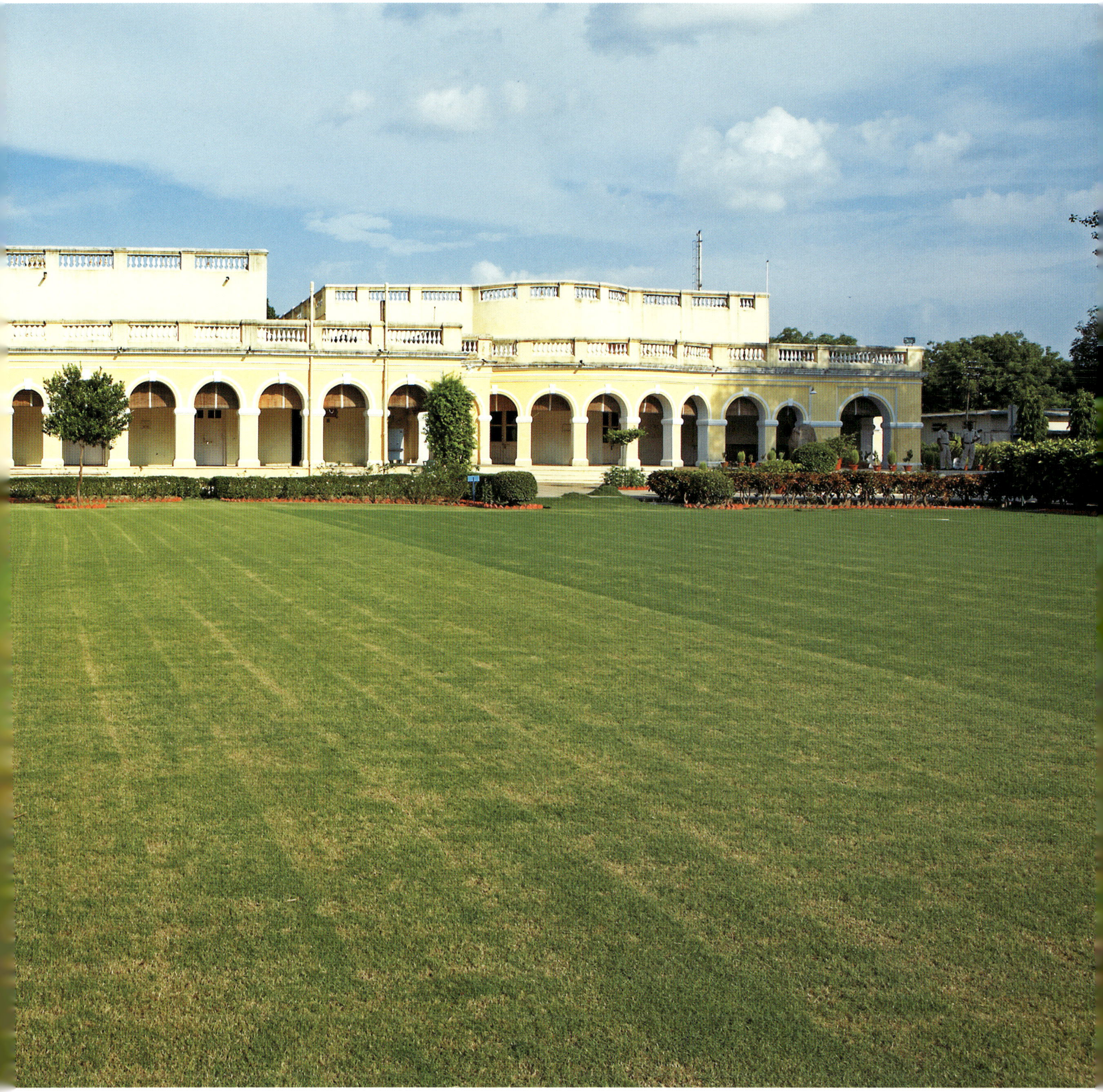

9
Portrait of Madan Mohan Malaviya, Allahabad's "elder statesman" of the freedom struggle and founder of the Banaras Hindu University. Courtesy Allahabad Museum.

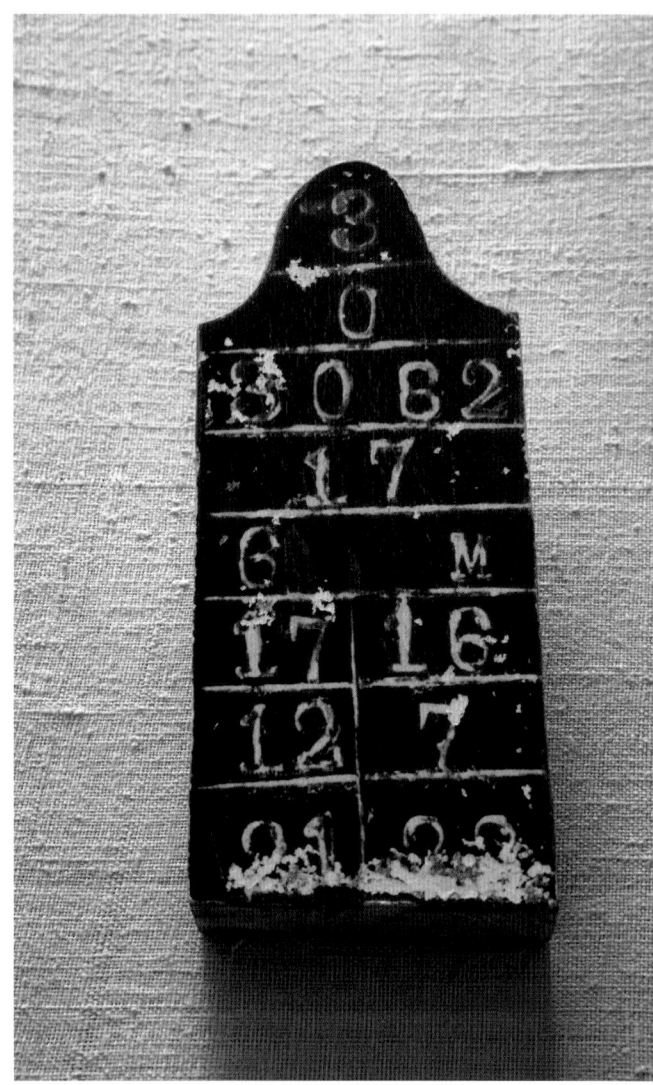

10
The wooden jail-ticket worn by Jawaharlal Nehru. Courtesy Anand Bhavan.

11 *opposite*
Anand Bhavan, Jawaharlal Nehru's home. The front balcony on the first floor was Mahatma Gandhi's meditation spot.

a carriage, and when it is pulled off, he swings," wrote Charles Ball (1860).

"Peppering away at niggers" as one English soldier put it, became a pleasant pastime. And "eight dead carts daily went their rounds from sunrise to sunset to take down the corpses which hung at the crossroads and marketplaces," according to Bholanath Chunder (1869). Citizens who tried to flee by boat across the rivers were fired upon from the Fort.

Independence

An uneasy lull followed 1857 and massive changes in British policy occurred which were turning points in Indian history. The rule of the East India Company ended and the British Crown took over the administration of India. Queen Victoria's famous "India shall be a jewel in our Crown" declaration was read out by Lord Canning as The Proclamation of Allahabad in 1858. The venue for the meeting was a stretch of land, much bruised and bloodied by recent events, on the bank of the Yamuna, where the razed Jami Masjid had once stood and which was named Minto Park and subsequently Madan Mohan Malaviya Park.

As the pulse of the freedom struggle quickened, Allahabad became the scene of a vibrant resistance movement involving the passions of the entire city. Activists of all persuasions operated – extremist or moderate, Congress or Forward Bloc. Dadabhai Naoroji's swaraj-mantra had impacted the city's imagination. Between 1905 and 1907 Lokmanya Tilak, Lala Lajpat Rai, Bipin Chandra Pal, and Gopal Krishna Gokhale addressed massive rallies in Allahabad. The movement drew not just eminent lawyers, high-profile public

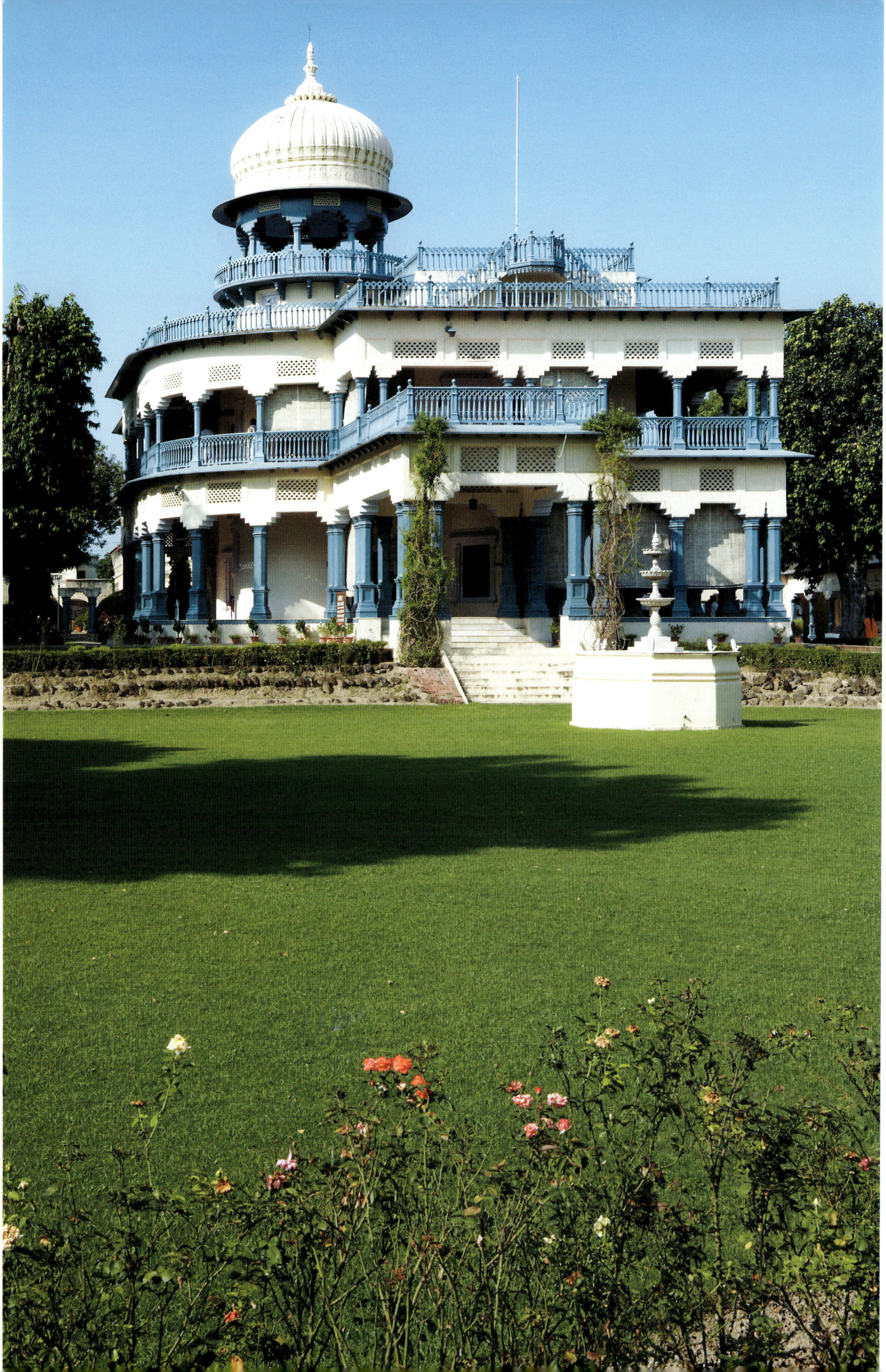

figures, and journalists, but also students, women, dalits, and other ordinary citizens as volunteers.

The first three sessions of the Indian National Congress, founded in 1885, met at Bombay, Calcutta, and Madras respectively. The fourth, in 1888, was at Allahabad, presided over by Sir Pherozeshah Mehta. The District Administration, as was customary, prevaricated in granting permission for the venue in an obvious effort to sabotage the event, but the Maharaja of Darbhanga rose to the occasion and specially purchased Lowther Castle for the event which turned out to be a grand one. Yet another annual Congress session was held here in 1892, presided over by W.C. Bonnerjee. The emergent local leadership comprised Pandit Bishambhar Nath, Ajodhya Nath, Madan Mohan Malaviya, Dr Surendranath Sen, and Motilal Nehru. 1910 witnessed the 25th session under the presidency of Sir William Wedderburn. In other annual sessions of the Congress held in other cities, leaders from Allahabad often presided – Madan Mohan Malaviya in 1907, 1909, and 1938; Motilal Nehru with active cooperation from Subhas Chandra Bose in 1928. Of special significance in national history are the 1919 session at Amritsar presided over by Motilal Nehru, held just after the Jallianwala Bagh massacre, and the historic Lahore session in 1929, when Jawaharlal Nehru famously demanded complete independence for India.

Alongside these moderate activists, the extremist presence in Allahabad was a powerful one. As early as 1894 one Ramnath Gupta had joined the Gadar Party at Vancouver, and Parmanand, another Gadar Party activist, was sentenced to 27 years' rigorous imprisonment. It is said that Bhagat Singh had hidden in a university hostel room here for some days and Ram Prasad Bismil escaped an attempt on his life in Allahabad. Rash Behari Bose, firebrand founder of the Azad Hind Fauj, hid in the kitchen of a school principal's house, dressed in a sari and chopping vegetables while the police and the CID combed the city for him. Two students from Allahabad were involved in the Multan

12
The room occupied by Mahatma Gandhi on his visits to Anand Bhavan. Courtesy Anand Bhavan.

96

BADRI NARAYAN TIWARI AND NEELUM SARAN GOUR

13
Conference hall in Anand Bhavan, scene of crucial discussions among national leaders. Inset shows Acharya Kripalani, Gandhi, and Rajendra Prasad in deep discourse. Courtesy Anand Bhavan and Teen Murti House.

Vande Bharatam

and Sholapur Conspiracy Cases and hanged. After the Alipore Bomb Case two activists, on Aurobindo Ghosh's instructions, operated in Allahabad – Satish Chandra Biswas and Jyotin Bose. Nityanand Chatterjee, disguised as a waiter, made an abortive attempt to throw a bomb at the British Governor at an event organized at the European Club, now the dilapidated building of the Cosmopolitan Club. Subhas Chandra Bose was given a rousing welcome in the city when he visited it and his Forward Bloc mission was ably carried on by the diligent Padmakant Malaviya. *Bomb Kya Hai* was the name of a popular poem by the dramatist-poet Madhav Shukla, a poem that unleashed great administrative fury. Sachindra Nath Sanyal and Bhupendra Nath Sanyal were associated with the Kakori Conspiracy Case and a certain Roshan Singh was hanged at the Malacca Jail. The gunning down of Chandra Shekhar Azad at Alfred Park in February 1931 is a stirring episode in the city's memory.

Meanwhile an office of Annie Besant's Home Rule League was established in Allahabad, ably led by Pandit Sunder Lal, Manzar Ali Sokhta, and Jawaharlal Nehru. A farmers' movement was started under Jawaharlal Nehru and Purushottam Das Tandon. The Jallianwala incident stirred up the city's indignation and the Congress plunged into a new phase of activism under Motilal Nehru and Madan Mohan Malaviya.

It was at the All India Khilafat Conference at Allahabad that Gandhi's

14
Motilal Nehru's sitting room.
Courtesy Anand Bhavan.

Badri Narayan Tiwari and Neelum Saran Gour

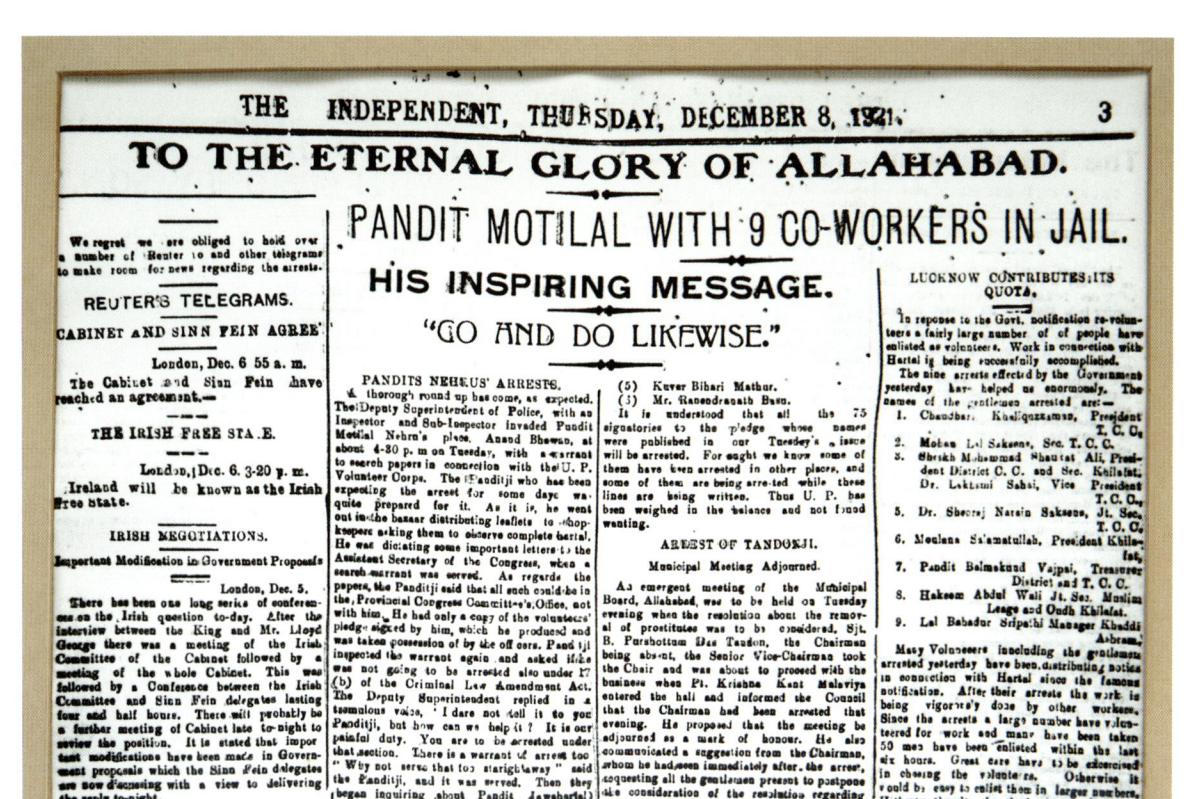

15
Privately printed journals played an active part in Allahabad's freedom movement. Reproduced is a sample page from Motilal Nehru's paper *The Independent* of December 8, 1921. Courtesy Allahabad Museum.

proposal for Non-Cooperation was aired. From then on Allahabad's history is interlocked with national history. From Non-Cooperation to Civil Disobedience to Quit India, it was a saga of satyagraha activism, rallies, bonfires, picketing, street fights, cavalry charges, proscribed making of salt, arrests, jail sentences, and torture. The two local jails, Naini and Malacca, housed thousands of satyagrahis and leaders whose names make up the chronicles of Indian nationalism and whose memoirs and books have become legendary.

A parallel leadership emerged under Purushottam Das Tandon, Acharya Narendra Dev, and Acharya Kripalani and was to influence people like Ram Manohar Lohia and Jai Prakash Narayan. The names of Govind Ballabh Pant, Kailash Nath Katju, Babu Shiv Prasad Gupt, and Venkatesh Narayan Tiwari are prominent among many others equally eminent and dedicated – too numerous to list here.

No account of the National Movement in Allahabad can overlook the many instances of volatile journalism that fuelled the fervour of the citizens. Journals like *Abhyudaya*, *The Independent*, *Deshbandhu*, *Karmayogi*, *Indian Herald*, *Indian Union*, *Hindustan Review*, *The Leader*, *Swarajya*, *Chand*, and *Bharat* carried on passionate critical polemics with the British administration and its spokespaper, *The Pioneer*. C.Y. Chintamani, Madan Mohan Malaviya, Padmakant Malaviya, Pandit Ajodhya Nath, Motilal Nehru, Thakur Srinath Singh, Sachchidanand Sinha, and Shanti Narayan carried activism from practice to print, articulating nationalist ideology in a time when printing anti-government material often had to be done at great risk, when newspapers had to keep changing their secret premises, when police

16
Jawaharlal Nehru with Indira and Feroze Gandhi and their son Rajiv, on the balcony of Anand Bhavan, 1945. Courtesy Anand Bhavan and Teen Murti House.

swoop-downs and arrests happened at the slightest hint of sedition, and newspaper offices often served as informal venues for activists to meet and plan strategy. Some fiery journalists like Shanti Narayan not only wrote, but personally printed, packed, and posted their papers. Many refused to apologize at their trials preferring to serve jail sentences. Journals frequently stopped publication and editors resigned on points of principle.

Activism was not confined to persons of high public visibility but involved anonymous people in the city and its encircling villages. Satyagrahis wanted by the authorities hid in private houses, university hostels, the homes of riverside *panda*s, and newspaper offices. When the Prince of Wales visited the city in 1921 most people stayed home in protest. When Krishnakant Malaviya's belongings were auctioned after his arrest, no buyers turned up, not even the *kabari*s, who buy and sell old goods. When Annie Besant, freshly released from prison, visited Allahabad in 1915, a hundred activists drew her carriage. When a general strike was declared after Gandhi's arrest in January 1932, police *sowar*s, mounted police, charged on a large crowd in Chowk, killing many. Women activists were particularly active during the freedom struggle, especially during the Salt Satyagraha. And there was a children's activism group too, known as the Vanar Sena, led by Indira, Jawaharlal's daughter. The contribution of unsung dalit activists is only now being recovered from local narratives by oral historians. The services rendered, the torture suffered, and the price paid by unknown activists like Ramadheen Patel and Girai Chamar of Shahabpur village are representative of a large body of forgotten or historically sidelined popular struggles by marginalized groups.

The National Movement fired the lives of citizens, students, peasants, and housewives, motivating two generations of Allahabadis, and constitutes the enduring stuff of the city's self-defining narrative. August 15, 1947 was celebrated with great enthusiasm. The Prime Minister of the new Indian Union was Jawaharlal Nehru with two eminent Allahabadis, Lal Bahadur Shastri and Keshav Dev Malaviya, as Railway

17
Indira Gandhi, Jawaharlal Nehru, Lal Bahadur Shastri, and K. Kamaraj. Courtesy Anand Bhavan and Teen Murti House.

Minister and Deputy Minister for Natural Resources, respectively. In the decades to follow Allahabad would supply Indian politics with five more Prime Ministers – Lal Bahadur Shastri, Indira Gandhi, Rajiv Gandhi, Vishwanath Pratap Singh, Chandra Shekhar – and several other key figures like Hemvati Nandan Bahuguna and Murli Manohar Joshi, through several successive chapters of India's experiments with a mutating democracy.

REFERENCES

Ball, Charles, *Indian Mutiny*, vol. I, London, n.d., 1860, pp. 253, 257.

Bholanath Chunder, *The Travels of a Hindoo*, 1869, cited in Kaye, *A History of the Sepoy War in India*, vol. II.

Campbell, George, *Memoirs of My Indian Career*, vol. I, Macmillan, London, 1893, p. 283.

Kaye, John William, *A History of the Sepoy War in India*, London, 1878. Colonel G.B. Malleson and a host of other British writers have written books about the rebellion of 1857 under this title.

Khan, Muinuddin Hasan, *Gadar 1857: An Eye-Witness Account*, translated into Hindi by Professor Abdul Haque, Hindi Madhyam Karyanvay Nideshalaya, Delhi University, 1999, pp. 99–102.

Malviya, Harimohan, "Swatantrata Sangram Mein Prayag ki Bhumika", *Prayag, Ateet, Vartaman aur Bhavishya*, edited by Badri Narayan Tiwari and Y.P. Singh, Vani Prakashan, Allahabad, 2003.

Mehta, Asoka, *The Great Rebellion*, Bombay, 1946, p. 60.

Pandey, Bishambar Nath, *Allahabad Retrospect and Prospect*, Allahabad Museum, 1955.

Russell, W.H., *My Diary in India in the Year 1858–59*, vol. II, 1860, p. 259.

Smith, Vincent A., ed. *Oxford History of India*, Oxford, 1981, p. 722.

Srivastava, S., *Prayag Pradeep*, Hindustani Academy, Allahabad, 1937, p. 58.

Hemendra Shankar Saxena

In Eastmancolor

Hemendra Shankar Saxena

"History is not so much what happened as what people said about it while it was happening," said the English historian G.M. Young (1882–1959). Insignificant incidents sometimes reveal a lot about the ethos of a people at a particular period. Civilizations are kept alive when certain values are created and recreated in men's minds. I remember some incidents which appeared to be of no consequence when they happened, but they could only have happened when they happened.

When I came to Allahabad in 1944 it was known as the "Oxford of the East", pulsating with hectic political and cultural activities. Within a radius of two kilometres there was the University Senate Hall, Muir Central College, Anand Bhavan, and the Public Library. It was said that if one threw a stone in this area it would hit a celebrity. Many students moved about with autograph books in their pockets. In August 1946 I purchased a copy of *The Discovery of India* and then, on an impulse, walked to Anand Bhavan to get it autographed by Pandit Nehru. Panditji was in a good mood and signed both in Hindi and in English. No one took particular notice of Professor N.R. Dhar rushing to the Chemistry Department of the University in a dressing gown, Acharya Kripalani haggling with the vegetable sellers in Colonelgunj, or the poet Nirala walking towards Firaq Saheb's residence at Bank Road with a big *rohu* fish dangling from his hand. Harivansh Rai Bachchan could be seen on the campus, cycling towards the English Department precisely at 9.45 am.

Both Firaq Saheb and Bachchanji taught English Literature at the University. Amaranatha Jha was the Vice-Chancellor. We were proud of our teachers. We felt that we were about to reach the end of an era and were on the threshold of another. It was the age of Gandhi and Tagore. Gandhi was not a person but a "climate of opinion". My narrative, however, is not hero-centric. I am writing about the common man on the streets of Allahabad and how he reacted to the great personalities of his city and the events of the age.

In March 1946 we had to appear for our BA examinations. On the eve of my examination I had a headache and high fever. I did not want to go to the University dispensary as it was quite far from my hostel. Someone suggested that I should go to the Congress dispensary, housed in a cottage near Swaraj Bhavan. During the Civil Disobedience Movement this modest dispensary was used as a hospital for injured Congress volunteers. Dr Mittra was the resident doctor. I walked to this dispensary alone and waited my turn as the doctor was busy with other patients. After some time he noticed me and asked me to lie down on a wooden

1 *opposite*
View of Sir Sunder Lal Hostel, Allahabad University.

2
An impromptu sketch, doodled by Saeed Jaffrey on a sheet of note-paper, of Professor K.K. Mehrotra, an erudite and popular don of the English Department at the Allahabad University. Courtesy Neelum Saran Gour.

bench. I looked around. The clinic was sparely furnished and khadi curtains hung at the windows. There was no portrait of Mahatma Gandhi on the wall, like we see in government offices and police stations today. But the Gandhian spirit was there. Dr Mittra felt my pulse and I mumbled something about my examinations. He administered a red mixture and asked me to wait. After some time he examined me again and told me to go back to my hostel and study. I got up and awkwardly took out a purse from my pocket. Dr Mittra flared up and shouted at me, "Thinking of money when you have to appear for your examination tomorrow? A student should only worry about his health and studies." He calmed down and after commenting on the poor state of my health, suggested that I should read Vivekanand during my summer vacations. I returned to my hostel happy and confident and studied European history with full concentration. This happened over 60 years ago. I do not remember what I studied that night but Dr Mittra's lecture on Vivekanand is still fresh in my memory. The environment of a city affects the mental development of young students. There were many people around us who inspired us to rise above parochialism, caste-prejudice, intolerance, and hatred. People like Dr Mittra demonstrated in their day-to-day dealings that they were completely in tune with Gandhian ideals.

A naive undergraduate from a small town used to keep the bathroom in our hostel occupied for a long time. It was the winter of 1944–45. There was no arrangement for hot water. Some students went without a bath for days. Those who wanted a bath had to take a shower early in the morning. It was discovered that this young man was talking to someone in the bathroom. We were curious. One of us peeped in. The tap was on and our friend stood half naked in a corner. He was talking to himself, "You are afraid of cold water. How can you drive out the British if you are afraid of cold water? Think of the plight of the Indian National Army in Burma ...." After some time he mustered up enough courage and, shouting Vande Mataram like a war-cry, jumped right under the running water. We laughed and laughed till our ribs ached. Our friend was a dreamer. We were all dreamers. I would like to quote a couplet by Firaq Saheb, our teacher: *Jao na is gumshudgi par hamare, ki har khwab se ek ahad ki buniyad pari hai* (Do not be misled by our absentmindedness or confusion – every dream lays the foundation of an epoch).

The curtain finally came down on the British Raj. Power was transferred to India at midnight, August 14/15, 1947. We could not listen to Nehru's famous "tryst with destiny" speech as we had no access to a radio-set. We were happy but not very demonstrative as we were psychologically not prepared for a truncated India, giving expression to our complex feelings in tawdry quotations from our classes. "Our sincerest laughter with some pain is fraught," an undergraduate quoted Shelley. A budding student leader retorted, "No use pining for what is not." Student leaders in those days delivered their speeches in English and had a sense of humour. One of them coined a slogan: "Let freedom won be freedom preserved." For Pandit Nehru had declared earlier, "We shall never allow the torch of freedom to be blown out, however high the wind, or stormy the tempest."

I remember some events that followed Independence Day celebrations. Political prisoners were released and some sort of amnesty was granted to other prisoners too. Students wanted clemency in examination results. So all students were awarded five or ten grace marks. Consequently some students who had failed were declared passed. This opened a Pandora's box. The next demand was that these lucky students should be admitted to the postgraduate classes. So the last date for admissions to the University was extended and the sanctity of the last date was lost for ever. One of my friends, who had, like many students, appeared in one or two papers, believing that he would not get a first division that year and tactically putting off the examination by another year, was also declared passed with a third division, thanks to "clemency". This was not what he wanted and he pleaded that he did not want any clemency. Those who had profited by clemency were nervous and argued that in a democratic, independent India all rules should be framed for the good of the majority. My friend was, by a special resolution, declared "failed", as he had wanted.

In 1948, another instance of attitudinal change occurred when a brilliant student who contested an election of the Students' Union lost because it was widely felt that a "bookworm" would not agitate for the good of "the majority". Cynicism had crept in and with it the growing power of mediocrity over excellence. Another question that agitated the minds of thinking people then was whether it was proper to agitate or apply satyagraha or go on a hunger strike on every trivial occasion. C. Rajagopalachari had warned at the very outset that civil

3
Kotwali Police Station a quarter-century ago. Courtesy John Harrison.

In Eastmancolor

ONKAR NATH RAJEEV GUPTA
COMPLETE SOLUTION FOR TRNASMISSION LINE
AUTHORISED DISTRIBUTOR
2 KVA - 500 KVA

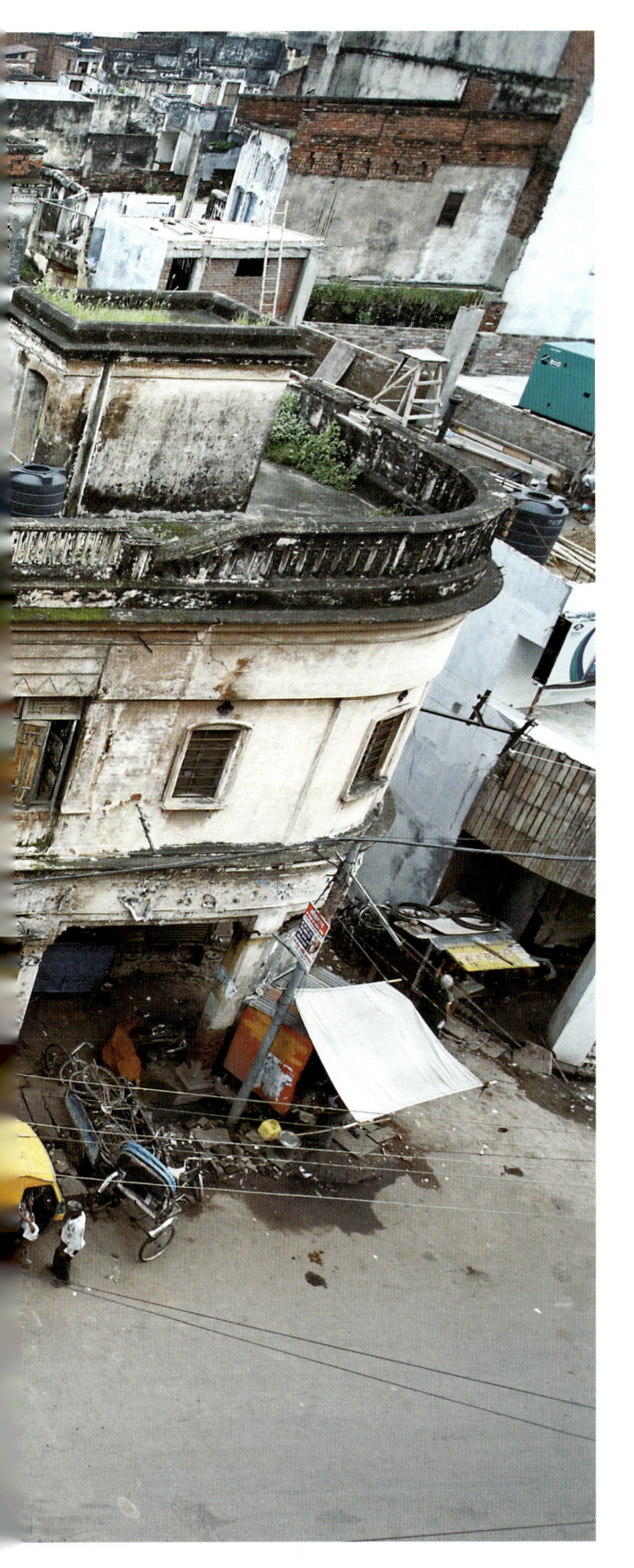

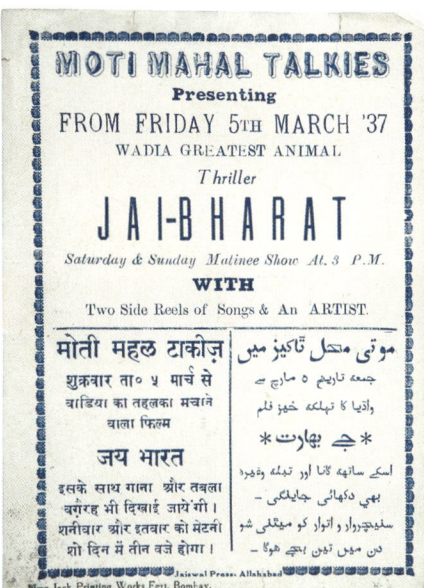

disobedience was different from criminal disobedience. But democracy was proving to be an open-ended system and new political ideals were in the making.

In the early '40s students, political leaders, and writers used to meet in restaurants on the University Road. Jagati's restaurant was already famous as Bhagwati Charan Varma had dedicated his novel *Teen Varsha* to Manohar Lal Sah Jagati, the proprietor. Bhagwati Babu was at the height of his popularity, the film version of his novel *Chitralekha* having been a hit. Moreover we had read his poems and short stories in Hindi textbooks along with those of Mahadevi Varma and Sumitranandan Pant. So, out of curiosity, we often went to this restaurant. Tea was served in a teapot and there were normally two cups of tea in the pot. One could get refills of boiling water free. After the first cup of strong tea, conversation was sustained by weaker cups. Later a part of this crowd shifted to the Indian Coffee House in the Civil Lines.

The Coffee House came into existence in August 1945 and became very popular with creative writers, academics, lawyers, and journalists after Independence. After the

5
A 1937 cinema-bill advertising a film running at Moti Mahal. The bill is worded in English, Hindi, and Urdu. Courtesy Neelum Saran Gour.

4 *left*
Moti Mahal Talkies, one of the city's oldest cinema halls (now closed down), which screened films for Indian audiences.

In Eastmancolor

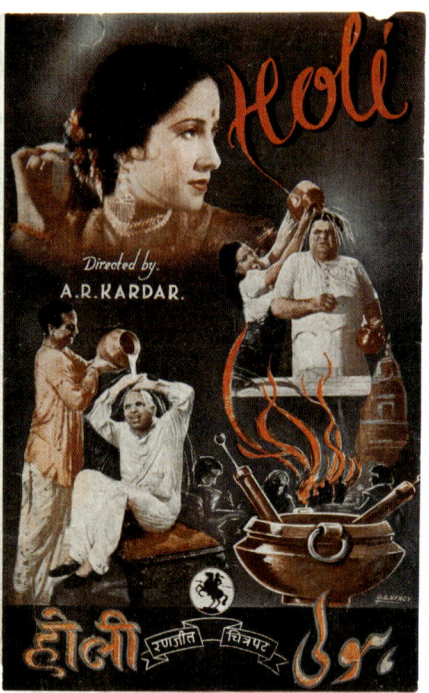

6
A 1940 cinema-bill advertising a film running at Vishwambhar Palace. Courtesy Neelum Saran Gour.

7
Vishwambhar Palace, also among the city's oldest movie halls and now closed down.

Partition many Hindi writers and scholars had settled in Allahabad as they found the intellectual climate of the city congenial to their unconventional attitude towards life and literature. Even senior poets and novelists like Ajneya and Bhagwati Charan Varma made it a point to visit the Coffee House when they were in Allahabad.

The Coffee House was first started in a spacious bungalow at the crossing of Clive Road and Canning Road (now Lohia Marg and Mahatma Gandhi Marg respectively). A large hall was tastefully furnished with comfortable chairs where one could sit and chat for hours over coffee. An adjoining room was reserved for "Ladies and Families". Another room near the kitchen was patronized by the more studious who wrote or studied with full concentration, undisturbed by the din and bustle of the main hall. Some young men even prepared for the Civil Service examinations in that room, which was cool and comfortable during the oppressive summer months. Coolers and air-conditioners were, of course,

IN EASTMANCOLOR

unheard of then. Some bohemians did not hesitate to have a wash under a shady tree in the backyard of the building, borrowing a towel or a duster from a friendly waiter. The Coffee House was like a colonial club but it lost some of its character when it shifted to its present site – Darbari Building.

Regular visitors to the Coffee House hailed the waiters by their first names. The waiters were smartly dressed in spotless white trousers, long coats, and starched turbans. The Head Waiter had a red and gold band round his waist while the others had green ones. They were mostly from Kerala and Tamil Nadu and this added to the cosmopolitan mélange of the Civil Lines. Most businessmen were Parsis and Gujaratis – Patels, Guzders, and Gandhis, to name a few. There were two Chinese shoe stores and a Bengali sweet shop. After the Partition they were joined by Punjabis. I vividly remember Mr Khanna of Law Books, nostalgically talking about his student days at Government College, Lahore.

Many apprentice *neta*s in white kurtas and pyjamas started visiting the Coffee

8
The famous Loknath shop of Hari Ram and Sons, makers and exporters of the well-known samosas, spiced-grams, and savouries of Allahabad.

Hemendra Shankar Saxena

House in the afternoons. Some pseudo-intellectuals carried impressive hardcover books and magazines. A young dilettante came to the Coffee House with a copy of Dostoevsky's *The Idiot* for three or four days consecutively. A senior Coffee House regular seriously advised him not to move about with his autobiography so openly. No one took offence at harmless banter. A student leader was merrily eating a mutton chop with a keen knife. Someone told him not to put the knife into his mouth and use the fork instead. He flared up, "These rules were made by the British. I do not care for them. I will eat with the knife and use it as a spoon." A waiter respectfully remarked, "Sir, you will cut your own tongue with that knife, not that of an Englishman."

Everybody laughed including that student leader who shook hands with the waiter.

The Coffee House played an important role in the academic and social circles of Allahabad. Anyone could join any group and take part in the thrust and parry of debate. These discussions were lively, provocative, and informative. Many major movements in Modern Hindi literature originated in Allahabad. More or less all creative writers, barring the very senior ones, visited the Coffee House. There was a table at the far end of the hall which was generally occupied by the members of the Parimal group and at the opposite end the Progressive Writers used to meet. Members of Parimal came daily while the leftists generally met on Saturdays. Many literary

9
A Loknath *rabriwala* hands an earthen bowl of the thick, sweetened milk-crust to a customer.

In Eastmancolor

I.C.W.CO.OP.SOCIETY LTD DELHI
INDIAN CoffEE HOUSE
इन्डियन काफी हाउस
P.C.DARBARI
PRASHANT DARBARI
15/29 M.G.MARG
NO SMOKING
UP-70
G-8108

magazines and journals like *Nayee Kavita, Naye Patte, Nikash* originated from these discussions in the Coffee House. There were differences but no bitterness. Prominent members of the Parimal group were Lakshmi Kant Varma, V.D.N. Sahi, Ram Swarup Chaturvedi, Dharamvir Bharati, Jagdish Gupt, Raghuvansh, and Sarveshvar Dayal Saxena. Regular members of the Progressive group were Bhairav Prasad Gupt, Amarkant, Markandeya, and Shekhar Joshi, who met once or twice a week. The Coffee House even hosted an art exhibition in which local painters were represented.

The Civil Lines market was lined with shady trees and many of the shops were located inside colonial bungalows with spacious lawns and guava orchards. One could walk at a leisurely pace from shop to shop. Once some students saw Sumitranandan Pant in a shop and overheard him asking for a "counterpane". The students did not know what a "counterpane" was and were intrigued. They consulted a dictionary that very evening and learnt that it was "an outer covering spread over bed clothes". They were thrilled that a great Hindi poet had added something to their English vocabulary and talked about this incident for days. Young students used to amuse themselves by mimicking their teachers, prominent political leaders, and film stars. Generations of students have mimicked Dr Ishwari Prasad's lectures on the French Revolution. Some backbenchers made sketches of their teachers and composed limericks. Here is a limerick by Dr Harivansh Rai Bachchan on Professor S.C. Deb. He composed it while an undergraduate:

> Professor Deb was the same in length
>   and breadth,
> And a man of encyclopaedic depth.
> He was humble to a fault
> And humbler to a somersault
> He could talk of Hafiz, Honolulu and
>   halwa in the same breath.

The presence of eminent people in our midst made us realize that education in the real sense lay in rising above arrogance and the lust for power and money. Our hopes for a bright future for India were not clouded by cynicism or doubt. We believed that a better quality of life for the common man was to come and our belief was founded on a way of life and examples of moderation and taste that were part of the air we breathed in Allahabad during the '50s.

10 *opposite*
The Indian Coffee House was a venue for intellectuals, lawyers, and politicians and has a rich store of literary anecdotage.

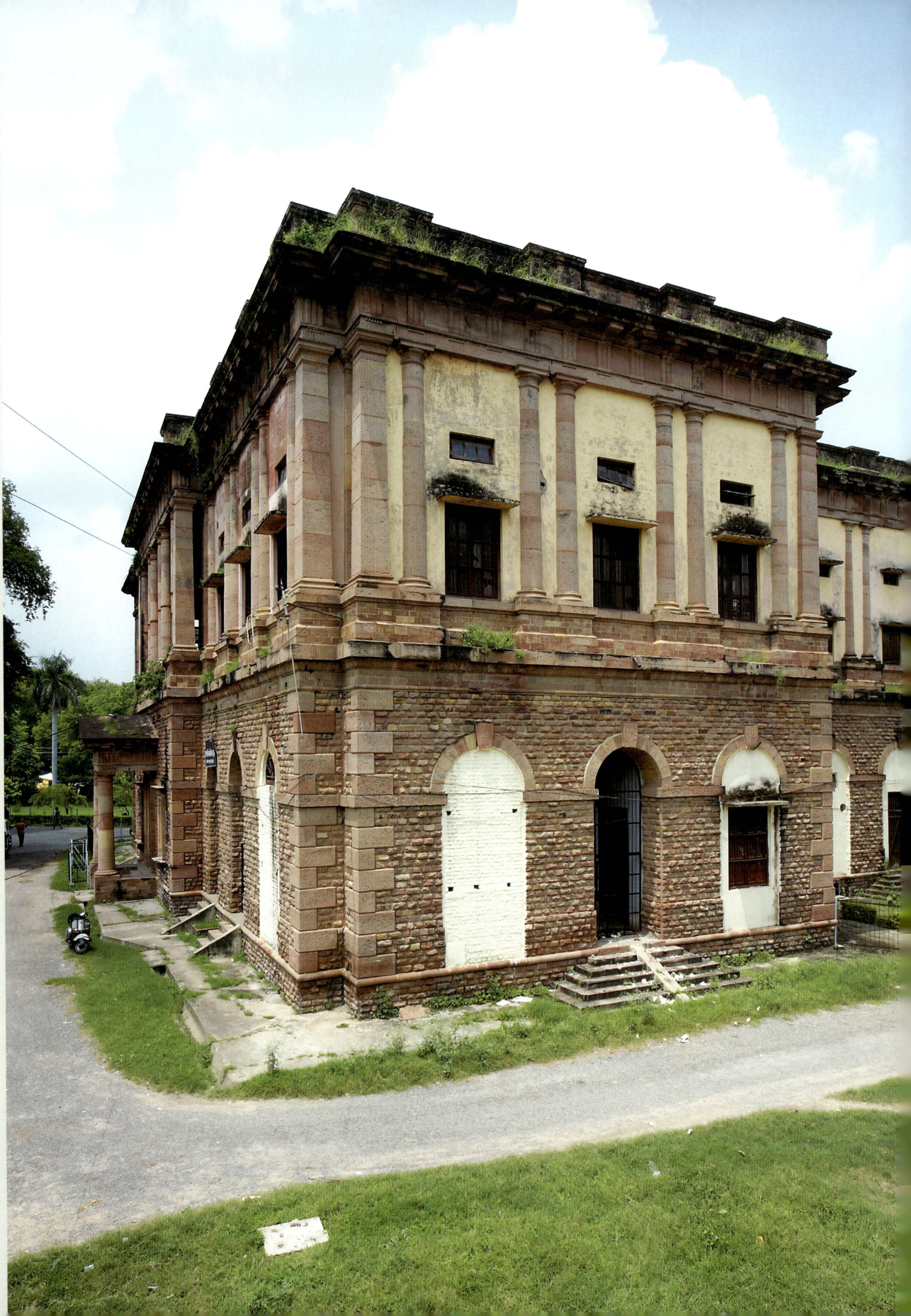

The Rule of Law

John Harrison

Allahabad lacks the cultural significance of Banaras for Hindus, of Agra, Delhi, or Lucknow for Muslims, and has never had the industrial importance of Kanpur. Its rank as one of the "big five" Uttar Pradesh cities it owes to the British who made it capital of a province and a major railway node. Muir Central College and Allahabad University became the most renowned training grounds in north India for Indians seeking higher employment in government and the professions. And in 1869 Allahabad acquired a High Court, the most important outside the presidency towns. Like the University it was a powerful anglicizing influence yet paradoxically one that fostered and provided leadership for Indian nationalism. The Court did so by upholding the rule of law under which Government and its officials themselves became subject to the law, and by fostering a professional body whose prestige and authority were largely independent of the executive government.

Background

Before 1857 the East India Company employed two types of court. For their European inhabitants in the three presidency towns there were Crown courts which for their laws, language, and judges looked to England and replicated its pattern of barristers and solicitors, adversarial procedures, and absolute outcomes in a world of contract rather than status. For their upcountry subjects, Indian and European, they created a series of courts, drawing on the Mughal inheritance. In the North-Western Provinces there were Munsif, Sadr Amin, and Principal Sadr Amin courts under Indian judges, and District and Sessions courts with British judges, with final appeal to Sadr Diwani and Nizamat Adalats, seated from 1834 to 1843 at Allahabad, thereafter at Agra. All these courts applied a mainly Muslim criminal law and in civil cases Muslim and Hindu personal law, modified by custom and Company regulations and otherwise as justice, equity, and good conscience might dictate.

Few barristers came further west than Patna, so that a body of Indian pleaders or vakils emerged to practise in the Company courts. From 1793 they were required to be "men of character and education, versed in the Mohammedan or Hindoo law and the Regulations", annually licensed. They were the product of Persian-language schools, since initially the court language was Persian, English having been rejected. This pattern continued even when Government, arguing that it was "easier for the judge to acquire the language of the people, than for the people to learn the language of the judge", switched to Urdu, for unhappily it was in the Persian script and so Persianized as to be equally foreign. Law classes were opened in the English-medium Government colleges at Agra and Delhi, but since their main text was Blackstone's *Commentaries* on English law they were useless to pleaders at the Adalat Courts.

1 *opposite*
The old Allahabad High Court building established in 1869 on Queen's Road, now Sarojini Naidu Marg.

It was not until 1852 that Sadr Court pleader examinations required some knowledge of English.

Then came 1857, the Crown assumed sovereignty, the East India Company vanished, and the Presidency Supreme Courts and the Sadr Adalats were alike swept away. Under the Indian High Courts Act of 1861 they were replaced by High Courts for the presidencies and in 1866 another for the North-Western Provinces to whose new capital, Allahabad, now rising like a garden city from the dusty uplands, it moved in 1869. There it occupied one of four severely handsome blocks astride Queen's Road (Sarojini Naidu Marg), officialdom's grand processional way. The Court had appellate jurisdiction over all lower courts of the province, but no original jurisdiction except in criminal cases against British-born subjects. The language of the Court was English; that of the lower courts, Urdu. Oddly, though Awadh had been annexed to the North-Western Provinces in 1856, the need to conciliate its great taluqdars after the Uprising led to Awadh

2
The new Allahabad High Court building inaugurated by Lord Chelmsford in 1916, on Nyaya Marg.

John Harrison

being given an independent executive, a Judicial Commissioner, and its own appeal court. Executive independence was surrendered in 1887, but the appeal court survived, even against the wishes of the Viceroy, Lord Curzon. It was only abolished after Independence, being replaced in 1948 by a divisional bench of the Allahabad High Court.

The High Court Bench

The composition of the High Court bench reflected its dual origins. Not less than one-third, the Chief Justice included, were drawn from the British Bars and as many again from the ICS. Initially the barristers were drawn directly from practice at home, conveyors, it was anticipated, of the ethos and high standards there. From the 1890s, however, it became usual to appoint barristers already practising at the Allahabad Bar, familiar with the work and language of the lower courts and High Court procedures. Some appointees had families long in Indian service: Edward Chamier's great-grandfather had been on the Madras Council and he had four serving brothers and two sisters in India, while there was always a Chichele Plowden somewhere in India from 1773 to 1947. For its ICS contingent the Court looked to senior District and Sessions judges. Their legal training as probationers was inadequate but they could claim direct experience of Indian life and vernaculars. Sir William Tudball is an example: "Typical ICS with brown moustache, cut to expose his upper lip, and keen penetrating eyes ... Tudball was well versed with local conditions, practices and customs. He was not very learned but was intelligent and had highly-developed commonsense." Sir Edward Bennett, though a keen shikari also "burnt the midnight oil and was uptodate on local laws".[1]

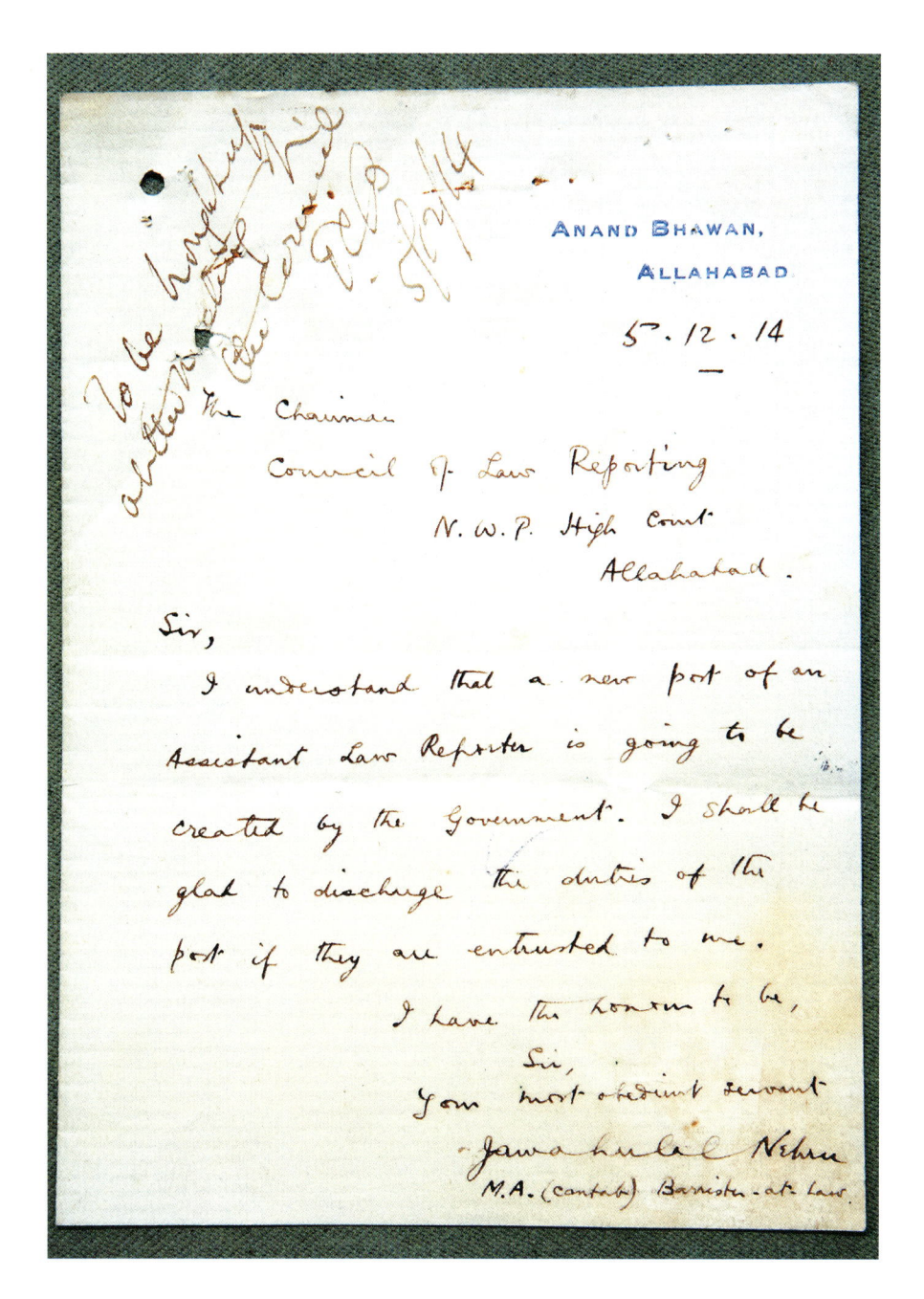

From 1886 men from the Provincial Judicial Service (PJS) were also eligible for High Court appointments. The Service was recruited from Indian Law graduates with at least three years of local practice, often expert in civil litigation, whereas ICS men, as magistrates, saw more criminal work. By 1912, of the 30 provincial District and Sessions judgeships eight were held by the PJS of whom two were elevated to the bench. Finally after 1896 the High Court

3
A letter written by Jawaharlal Nehru, applying for a job at Allahabad High Court. Courtesy Allahabad High Court Museum.

HIGH COURT

could elect distinguished vakils of ten years' standing to the rank of barrister/advocate, thus eligible for a seat on the bench. In 1916 Sunder Lal Dave was so elevated.

In 1866 the salary of a puisne judge was set at the attractive figure of Rs 3,750 a month, with a generous pension at 60, though with a ban upon returning to practice after retirement. But with its value eroded by income tax, and from 1914 by war-time inflation, it came to prove less attractive to British barristers for whom an Indian career, with the tide of nationalism rising, seemed less secure. However, there were Indian barristers too and in 1887 Syed Mahmud, son of loyalist Syed Ahmad Khan, became the first Indian High Court judge at Allahabad. His obvious successor was a Bengali – but Congress was disturbingly active in Bengal. The Lieutenant-Governor, Crosthwaite, warned the Viceroy in 1895: "to appoint a Bengali ... may please the advanced Congress party, who would rather see a Chimpanzee on the bench than an Englishman. It will please no-one else."[2] He was rebuffed, for it was Pramode Charan

4 *opposite*
Allahabad High Court, view of the facade.

5
The Marble Hall and the famous heritage grilles in the High Court.

THE RULE OF LAW

6
Panel bearing portraits of famous High Court judges. Courtesy Allahabad High Court Museum.

Banerji, PJS, who succeeded Syed Mahmud. Both were admirable choices, their legal acumen applauded on all sides. But the provincial government continued its search for politically "safe" men. The High Court itself protested at "safe" but sometimes mediocre choices, but in vain.

High Court Practitioners
a) Barrister-advocates

Like the judges, the practitioners at the new High Court reflected their dual origin. One Armenian and just five European advocates together with 37 pleaders moved from the old *adalat*s to Allahabad. By 1875, 29 more European advocates had been enrolled, many from old service families: G.T. Spankie and G.E.A. Ross were sons of High Court judges, while C.M. Dick's father was a general, retired in Mussoorie. Such men were at ease socially, knew the vernaculars, and had useful local contacts to build a practice on. (Litigants sometimes assumed that they would have the ear of British judges.) Of those who came out but lacked those advantages, few succeeded at Allahabad – Charles Ross Alston, the son of a Glasgow merchant being an able exception. The unsuccessful left Allahabad to serve the European communities in Calcutta, the industrialists at Kanpur, or the property owners in the hill stations. The Armenian H.W. Arathoon and the Eurasian Ernest David succeeded because each had a communal niche to occupy.

Initially most advocates were European. Between 1866 and 1886, while 64 Europeans enrolled only four Hindus and nine Muslims did so. This was a measure of the cost to Indians of three years at the Inns of Court in London, but even more of the religious problems posed to both communities. The England-returned Hindu barrister, even after elaborate purification ceremonies suffered some social ostracism. Sachchidanand Sinha and some early Bengali barristers migrated to Allahabad to escape this. It was such men who promoted the Anglo-Bengali School and Kayastha Pathshala to encourage acceptance of English language and ideas, as Muslims did in founding Aligarh College. They succeeded: from 1908 to 1928, 80 Muslims and 83 Hindus became advocates of the High Court; just 13 Europeans. While British barristers dominated on the criminal side, where eloquence rather than local connections mattered, Indians did so on the civil side.

b) Vakils

Just two European vakils made the move from Agra to Allahabad. Four years later there were 23 European and Eurasian vakils, mainly college graduates, for since 1857 Law had become an approved second degree in the affiliated colleges of the new Calcutta University. (Becoming an LLB was thus a lengthy process, involving study of both English and Law, but the reward was automatic admission as a pleader.) However, by 1895, of the 23 only two survived – J. Simeon, the Eurasian President of the Allahabad Vakils Association, and his son J.J. Simeon. Later poor Eurasians lacked any vakil of their own community until the teacher O.M. Chiene took up the law. Few of the prosperous Persian-educated Muslims of the Sadr Adalats made the transition to the High Court. Vastly over-represented at Agra they were out of favour after the Mutiny and occupied a modest position at Allahabad. The Bengalis, by contrast, who had earlier acquired English in Bengal, found new opportunities at the High Court.

Law classes were opened in Muir Central College and in 1872 a separate Law College, its numbers boosted from 1877 by the High Court's requirement that all candidates for the Vakils Examination must have attended law classes. Muir early produced a bevy of prominent Bengali successes, notably S.C. Banerji and S.N. Sen, whose academic brilliance took them to the top. (Surendranath Sen, LLD, rose to the High Court bench.) The traditional writer caste, the Kayasthas, also flourished. Munshi Hanuman Prasad built up a fine High Court practice to which his son Madho Prasad, his nephew Gokal Prasad, and his grandson Ambika Prasad, later president of the Allahabad Bar Association, all succeeded. Narayan Prasad Asthana and Iswar Saran were others of great distinction, the latter especially on the criminal side.

But the most spectacular success was achieved by a handful of English-knowing Kashmiri and Nagar brahmin families, formerly in Mughal service and fluent in Urdu, who could straddle the gap between Muslim and Hindu society. The Kunzrus from Agra, the Chak and Nehru families from Kanpur, and the Dhar, Mulla, and Gurtu families from Lucknow, where Jagat Narain Mulla was the leading criminal

7
The lion and the unicorn crest, insignia of the British Crown, which adorned the facade of the High Court building till Independence. Courtesy Allahabad High Court Museum.

THE RULE OF LAW

lawyer, all thrived at the High Court, while Tej Bahadur Sapru would rise to be Law Member in the Viceroy's Council in 1920. With Motilal Nehru, he was deeply respected by other Kashmiri brahmins – the Zutshis, Mushrans, and Katjus.

Four Nagar brahmin Dave brothers moved to Allahabad when the High Court did so. One became Judicial Commissioner of Awadh, while Sunder Lal Dave built an enormous first appeal practice and became the first vakil to be elevated to the High Court bench. He served as Vice-Chancellor at Allahabad and with Madan Mohan Malaviya tirelessly promoted Banaras Hindu University, of which he was first Vice-Chancellor.

Building a High Court Practice

What was needed to succeed at the High Court? One short answer was money, money to carry the young hopeful through a BA and an LLB and for an office in which to work and interview clients – preferably a room at home or with a relative, if not a hired room or shed near the Court. (House-owners in the Civil Lines made a steady income from such lettings.) Only the hard-pressed met their clients under a tree or an umbrella. While Indian dress was appropriate in the district courts, by the 20th century men like Durga Charan Banerji affected full European dress, undeterred by Gandhi's khaddar movement. Similarly, travel to court by bullock cart might do in Hamirpur, a tonga in Kanpur, but in Allahabad a smart phaeton, or by 1910 a car, was in fashion: Motilal and Sunder Lal kept both. The young entrant needed copies of the Codes of Criminal and Civil Procedure, frequently revised, and, because case law had become increasingly important, runs of the Indian Law Reports,

which cost Rs 1,000 and needed constant updating. For many this meant saving for years. The very successful Sunder Lal held full runs of Reports – Sadr Adalat, All-India, Agra and other High Courts, as well as English, Irish, and American Law Reports. Finally, money was needed to live on in the long lean early years.

A High Court lawyer-father might take a son under his wing but the usual route to acquiring funds to start at the High Court was a career in the district courts. Living was cheaper, the family was known, marriage and caste ties extended a potential network of contacts. Funds and clients so accumulated could then back the gamble of a move to the High Court.

In England country solicitors fed briefs to the barrister and met the pupils who were training with him. No such system existed at Allahabad. Moreover, established lawyers in India were very unready to take a junior who was not a relative: Mr Justice Stuart commented sadly, "The view of the legal profession is that it is bad business to instruct a possible rival."[3] A good practice was a family inheritance which it was a duty to preserve. Nor was the process of "taking silk" introduced which barred seniors from taking private cases of modest value. At Allahabad even the most successful would take such cases if the fees (*shukrana*s) were fat enough. This allowed a small number of leaders to create immense practices stretching deep into the hinterland, but left large numbers at the High Court struggling to survive.

Their situation was worsened by the flow of law graduates from the new universities springing up in the 1920s across the province, each with its own law college. The disappointed and disgruntled turned to politics. The few posts government could

8
Portrait of Queen Empress Victoria and the Royal Charter establishing the Allahabad High Court. Courtesy Allahabad High Court Museum.

offer – judgement-writer, law-reporter, or government advocate – being politically sensitive, went to Europeans. Happily, when government asked the High Court to threaten lawyers who meddled in politics it stoutly refused, jealous as always of its independence: "The members of the bar in this province are not given to disloyalty, though they, European as well as Native freely criticize the Government and its measures."[4] In reality few lawyers responded in a more than token way to the call for Non-Cooperation; even Motilal put duty to his family before that to the Swaraj Fund.

The High Court's Letters Patent of 1866 had provided for a Chief Justice and five puisne judges. That soon proved insufficient, as did the two further judgeships secured by 1906. The First World War caused further disruption, so that when Sir Grimwood Mears came out as Chief Justice in 1919 he was horrified by the arrears. By 1922 they had been cleared, the judges working very long hours, with holidays, he complained, much shorter than in England with its cool nights of sleep, "unbroken by brain-fever birds, koels and frogs". However, his success was short-lived, for first appeals were increasing by 500 a year and by then the nationalist movement had moved from protest to direct action. The Chauri-Chaura conspiracy case appeals in 1923 occupied two senior Allahabad judges for some 40 working days and created a record backlog of unheard cases. By Order in Council, the bench was enlarged in 1935 to a maximum of 12 puisne judges.

If the initial bench was early outgrown, so was the first High Court building. The foundation stone of the present Court on Hastings Road was laid in 1911 and by 1916 the new building with its double roof of Frizzoni tiles was open. Additional wings have since been added, embracing its garden and fountains. Judges upon appointment were still required to find their own housing in the Civil Lines, inspecting such bungalows as were available, their household belongings following on *thela* or bullock cart. The great merchant-banker "Bachchaji" at one time had eight judges as his tenants. It was not much later that the present judges' quarters were built.

Today, Uttar Pradesh is no longer a purely agrarian state, the pressure of land revenue has been eased, and, more importantly, there is no alien government using the courts to impose a foreign concept of property upon a resisting countryside. New waves of litigation have been excited by zamindari abolition and land-ceiling legislation, but land is no longer the sole issue. Commercial and industrial growth have thrown up their own issues in contract and labour law, as also in taxation, income-tax in particular. And the High Court has been charged with new duties under the Constitution: the protection of individual human rights and the upholding of the Constitution itself. To many, however, the High Court's most important act was taken in June 1975 when it struck down the election of Prime Minister Indira Gandhi.

It did so hesitantly and timidly, but it did so, and in so doing upheld that Rule of Law upon which the Constitution stands.

Lawyers played a major role in securing Indian Independence and democracy. Motilal provided driving force, while it was Sapru, with his belief in constitutional methods and his upbringing within the syncretic north Indian Mughal culture which allowed him to keep Muslim and Hindu delegates to the Round Table Conferences united, who secured the 1935 Act which made Independence inevitable. The Allahabad High Court can be proud of these champions. The question in 1947 was whether the political forces which it helped unleash would build upon their work or destroy it.

Part of the answer came in June 1975 when subsequent to the judgement of Justice J.M.L. Sinha against Prime Minister Indira Gandhi, which rendered her official position as Prime Minister infructuous, she chose to declare a state of internal emergency rather than resign. The Emergency is remembered as one of the darkest chapters in modern Indian history, a contravention of much that democracy meant and the Constitution promised. Specifically it involved the enforcement of the Maintenance of Internal Security Act or MISA as it was notoriously known. Under the guise of precautionary preventive detention thousands of people were arrested without warning and detained without trial. Disappearances and torture of teachers, journalists, political activists and workers, and anybody perceived as a threat were frequent. India functioned as a police state for 21 months and it was in this context that the Habeas Corpus Case arose. With thousands of detenues languishing in jail and Article 359 of the Constitution suspended, the right to appeal

9
Motilal Nehru driving Allahabad's first motor car. Vijayalakshmi and Krishna are in the back seats. Courtesy Allahabad Museum.

to the courts was denied and by reason of this denial Article 21 of the Constitution guaranteeing the right to life and liberty was also suspended – a flagrant violation of one of the first principles of natural justice. The question central to any democracy, whether appeals from detenues could or could not be heard as cases of Habeas Corpus, became a national issue during the 21 months of the Emergency.

The Allahabad High Court, along with certain other High Courts in the country, decided that the Habeas Corpus petitions were maintainable. A mood of defiant activism prevailed in the High Court, although there were sections that stayed cautiously compliant and therefore complicit. But many committed lawyers appeared for relief of detenues, often without charging a fee or at a nominal charge. And although the Habeas Corpus Case was dismissed by a panel of Supreme Court judges, it marks a strong and principled stand of the High Court at Allahabad in opposition to an authoritarian regime.

If governments could be unseated and thrown into defensive overreaction by a decision of the Allahabad High Court, a state government could be reinstated by a lightning decision of the Court, as happened in the case of the Kalyan Singh ministry which was recalled to power in UP in February 1998.

Questions of judicial activism and the contending powers of judiciary and executive continue to be argued back and forth, a legacy of those times when executive decree first established a High Court in the North-West Provinces and subsequently, and ironically, supplied some of the leading dissenters against the executive machinery. Dissent was and is the prevailing disposition of the city of Allahabad and the High Court has done much to foster the city's argumentative spirit.

NOTES

1   Narmadeshwar Upadhyaya, "Snippets from Memory", in *Centenary High Court of Judicature at Allahabad 1856–1966, Commemoration Volumes*, vol. II, Allahabad, 1966.

2   Crosthwaite to Viceroy Lansdowne, September 17, 1895, *Lansdowne Correspondence*, vol. III, no. 260, quoted in G.F.M. Buckee's "An Examination of the Development and Structure of the Legal Profession at Allahabad, 1866–1935", unpublished PhD thesis, 1972.

3   Mr Justice Stuart, "Note of 15th September, 1919" – Home Judicial deposit, November 1920, no. 4, National Archives of India.

4   Chief Justice Sir Grimwood Mears to Secretary to UP Government, July 3, 1925 – Home Judicial deposit, 1925, no. 588, National Archives of India.

Manas Mukul Das

Banyan Tree

Manas Mukul Das

Perhaps the first function of a university is the making of the human mind: a larger collective consciousness, which is the aroma or the soul of the university, pervading all spheres of human endeavour, as well as multitudes of individual minds spread over generations. When I was asked to write about the University of Allahabad, my alma mater and place of work, I looked for the intangible University. Not the postal address, the mere infrastructure of grounds and buildings, administrative offices, library, and laboratory, nor the structure of Acts, Statutes, and Ordinances, but the source of the creative energy that shapes minds. My first impression of the University persists as a vast space of majestic shady trees and beautiful stone and brick buildings with canopies and balconies, high doors and windows with shimmering ribbed-glass panes, and a domed tower with clocks facing four directions and a hidden bell, striking every quarter hour, rolling its chimes down to far distances.

For me it has been a campus of continually changing foliage, flowers, barks, shadows, fragrances, and the whispers of trees, at different times of the day and the year, all of which have feasted the senses and connected the mind to the flow of a vast energy of renewal. One moved about the campus surrounded by a sense of grace and benediction. Which takes me back to a day when, as a very young person, I was admiring a Kachnar in bloom in the almost deserted Arts Campus. I did not notice an elderly person with a walking stick in one hand and smoking a pipe with the other, till he came quite close, looked at me with merry, mischievous eyes, and asked, "Young man, what are you admiring?" Taken aback, I fumblingly told him that I thought the Kachnar flowers were beautiful. He asked me, "Have you noticed the shape of the leaves and the colour and feel of the bark, the proportions of the trunk and branches?" Then he took me around to show me more trees, tell me their names and all about them. "The wind makes beautiful sounds passing through leaves of different shape, size, and thickness. It is a delight to listen to them separately and together. Very early in the morning, before daybreak, there is more moisture in the air and the soft sounds are clear and undisturbed. You can hear a leaf fall, a drop of dew, a cat over leaves. A little later the place is full of bird sounds." I did not know who he was. Later, however, I came to know him well. He taught English literature and was also a painter – some of his paintings hang in the National Gallery of Modern Art in New Delhi. One day when a mob of agitating, slogan-shouting students set fire to a curtain, I saw him face the mob, take off his coat, and beat down the flames with it. From him, more than anyone else perhaps, I learnt what a teacher should be. I learnt that a university is a fraternity of teachers and students and not a knowledge market. The Allahabad University, as I knew it, was full of majestic trees, buildings, and personalities.

1 *opposite*
Allahabad University's central symbol, the famous banyan tree representing the city of the *akshaya-vat* and the dissemination and expansion of learning through each aerial root. Photograph: Devanshu Gour.

The Senate House

The historic Senate House commands the Arts Campus. Built shortly before the First World War, when the British empire was at the height of its power, it blended elements from Islamic, Rajasthani, and English styles of architecture, to stand as an icon of order and imperial authority. The perfect symmetry of the consolidated design of three buildings in a row converges on a central clock-tower, which from its height sonorously and emphatically announced, not only the hours, but also the quarter, half, and three-quarters with rolling chimes. In this complex of buildings, Sir Swinton Jacob, the architect, visualized a blending of space and time, a mingling of the symmetry of pattern with the regularity of rhythm. The order, repetition, and balance of motifs within a spatial design were being continually reinforced every quarter hour by the regularity and sequence of the beats and melody in the chimes of a hidden bell situated high in the centre of the tower. The symmetrical external form emblemized the perfect order in which an unseen centre held together its spacious domain. Seen from inside, before the archways connecting the Central Hall to the North and South Halls of the main building were sealed, as they are now, the Senate House building was one integrated flowing space that provided a magnificent aspect of vistas within vistas of archways, halls, balconies, overhanging galleries, and connecting bridges with latticed stone railings, pillars and arches, deep verandahs from which carved stone staircases ascended to the first floor, ceilings decorated with carved woodwork, light filtering through stained-glass designs set in huge skylights, polished red floors embellished with mosaic patterns, and rows of tall, brass-fitted, teakwood and ribbed-glass windows and doors opening onto a view of meadows, trees, paths, and adjoining peer buildings. Looking at the changing vistas, through arches within arches within arches, one got the feeling that the domain of knowledge was the unknown, unfolding as one passed through the arches into a forever receding horizon. Today the chimes are silent, a number of arches sealed, the texture of stone and exposed brick surfaces hidden under coats of paint. Moulded plastic chairs are screwed onto the red floor. Wire mesh and asbestos partitions divide several halls into cubicles for the administrative staff. Still the desecrated buildings retain much of their grandeur.

In fashioning the Senate Hall like a durbar hall, Sir Swinton Jacob might have intended observers to associate the order and authority it symbolized with the British empire. The University community accorded scant respect to the empire. When the Prince of Wales visited Allahabad in January 1921, a stage-managed official reception was organized in the Senate Hall, barely a decade after it was built. The Governor and the Vice-Chancellor welcomed the Prince and introduced him to the executive councillors in an almost empty hall. The students and citizens observed a total boycott. The Muir College sports over which the Prince was to have presided were cancelled. The Prince recorded later in his memoirs: "When on the appointed day I emerged from the train, in full dress uniform, and started off from the railway station in a state carriage, it was to be met in the native city by shuttered windows and ominous silence along with troop lined, deserted streets. It was a spooky experience. I attempted to maintain a rigid and majestic pose in the carriage in order to show that I had risen above the insult."[1]

Muir College

While the architecture of the Senate House blended the pattern of space and the rhythm of time to symbolize order and authority, far more profound symbolically are the dome, the tower, and the inner courtyard of the Muir College connected to the vast emptiness of the sky. The two architectures reflect different attitudes of the empire towards India at different points of time.

In 1858, just after India's First War of Independence, or Uprising, the British shifted the capital of the then North-West Provinces from Agra to Allahabad. In 1872 the Muir Central College, which later would house and then merge with the University of Allahabad, started functioning in rented accommodation, affiliated to the University of Calcutta. Plans were underway to provide the college with worthy premises. *The Pioneer* of December 3, 1873, said, "The Muir Central College, the foundation stone of which is to be laid by the Viceroy this afternoon, will be, we are assured, when completed, the finest structure in the N.W. Provinces, except only the Taj." The Queen of England's government in India, through the architecture of its public buildings, was trying to speak to a subject nation that had only recently risen in revolt against the rule of the East India Company. Care had been taken not to disturb sentiments, to extend a gesture of goodwill, and to surpass the architectural grandeur of the past. Instead of the Gothic, Sir William Emerson chose "a modified Saracenic style" of architecture for the college building which took a little over 12 years to complete. At its formal opening on April 8, 1886, Sir Alfred Lyall, Governor of the province, said in his speech:[2]

> Now that we have taken to erecting for our students a hall like this in which we are assembled, with cool colonnades, domes, and towers, spacious lecture rooms and libraries, we have set up an external visible sign of the spirit in which our generation regards education. We are giving expression … to the ancient feeling that architecture may play a great part in education, and that knowledge, like other powerful influences, should have a fitting seat and sanctuary.

By choosing the language of the Islamic tradition of architecture, William Emerson erected a building that perhaps said more than he was aware of consciously. At the height of its glory, Islamic culture was a synthesis of Arab vigour and Persian grace. Rejecting the very thought that the splendour of Godhead can at all be represented through finite natural forms, Islam developed an abstract, austere art. The tower in Islamic architecture emphasized the gesture towards the Infinite, the upward thrust, the vertical axis connecting the human to the divine. From the tower the Muslim proclaimed the greatness of Godhead and called man to prayer. What if the arrogant empire flew the Union Jack on the tower? The dome was the perfect form symbolizing harmony and grace. The tiles that covered it were lustre-painted and polished to mirror the infinite sky, creating an optical illusion of transforming the density of light, symbolically enacting the transmutation of matter into spirit, dark ignorance into wisdom. While the tower pointed to the infinite, the dome absorbed and interiorized it. Over the centuries, long, broad verandahs surrounding an inner space, symbolically the cave of the heart, have been used for reading, prayer, and meditation while walking. An inner courtyard, connected to the sky, invites the infinite to the centre of a community's

2 *below*
The Muir College tower and dome before disfigurement of the tiles. Courtesy John Harrison.

3 *opposite*
The Muir College tower and dome, a contemporary image.

dwelling place and all its activities. Alumni from early days of the Muir Central College, in their memoirs, have recalled Professors Thibaut and Homersham Cox, sometimes silent, sometimes lost in dialogue, walking together up and down under the arches of stone-paved verandahs surrounding three and a half sides of its immense inner court, green under a blue sky.

The tiles on the dome of the Vizianagram Hall were glazed by craftsmen belonging to Rajasthan guilds which for several generations had preserved the centuries-old secret of the art of glazing tiles, an art that had moved out of Egypt with Cairo potters migrating after the fall of the Fatimid dynasty in 1171. It flourished and developed under the Seljuk Turks in Iran and Anatolia; the Atabek and Ayyubid dynasties in Iraq, Syria, and Egypt; the Mongol, the Timurid, and the Safavid dynasties in Central Asia and Iran; the Mamluks in Egypt, the Nasrids in Spain, and the Ottoman Turks in Anatolia. It decorated masjids, madrasas, and mausoleums in famous Central and West Asian cities. From there it came to the Mughal courts and Rajasthan. When Sir William Emerson thought of glazed tiles for the Muir College dome, Rajasthan guilds were entrusted the job of lustre-painting imported tiles. The artisans still kept their knowledge secret. A beautiful dome was built which many living today have seen and remember. The glazed tiles reflect every mood of the sky. Bright and austere in the heat of midsummer afternoons, the dome was dreamy and mystic on full-moon winter nights, and sombre and brooding when clouds gathered. Those tiles are gone. A thoughtless vice-chancellor in the 1980s hired labourers who, armed with chisels, demolished these lovely products of an 800-year-old lost tradition of tile-glazing. Another vice-chancellor had the natural yellow and white stone, brought originally from Mirzapur and Sheorajpur, painted pink and brown. A similar fate befell the Senate House buildings. Today, the austere dignity and aristocracy of stone lie covered in paint. When the Muir College premises had been built, against wall spaces created for them, mahogany bookshelves had been fitted into notches carved for their support

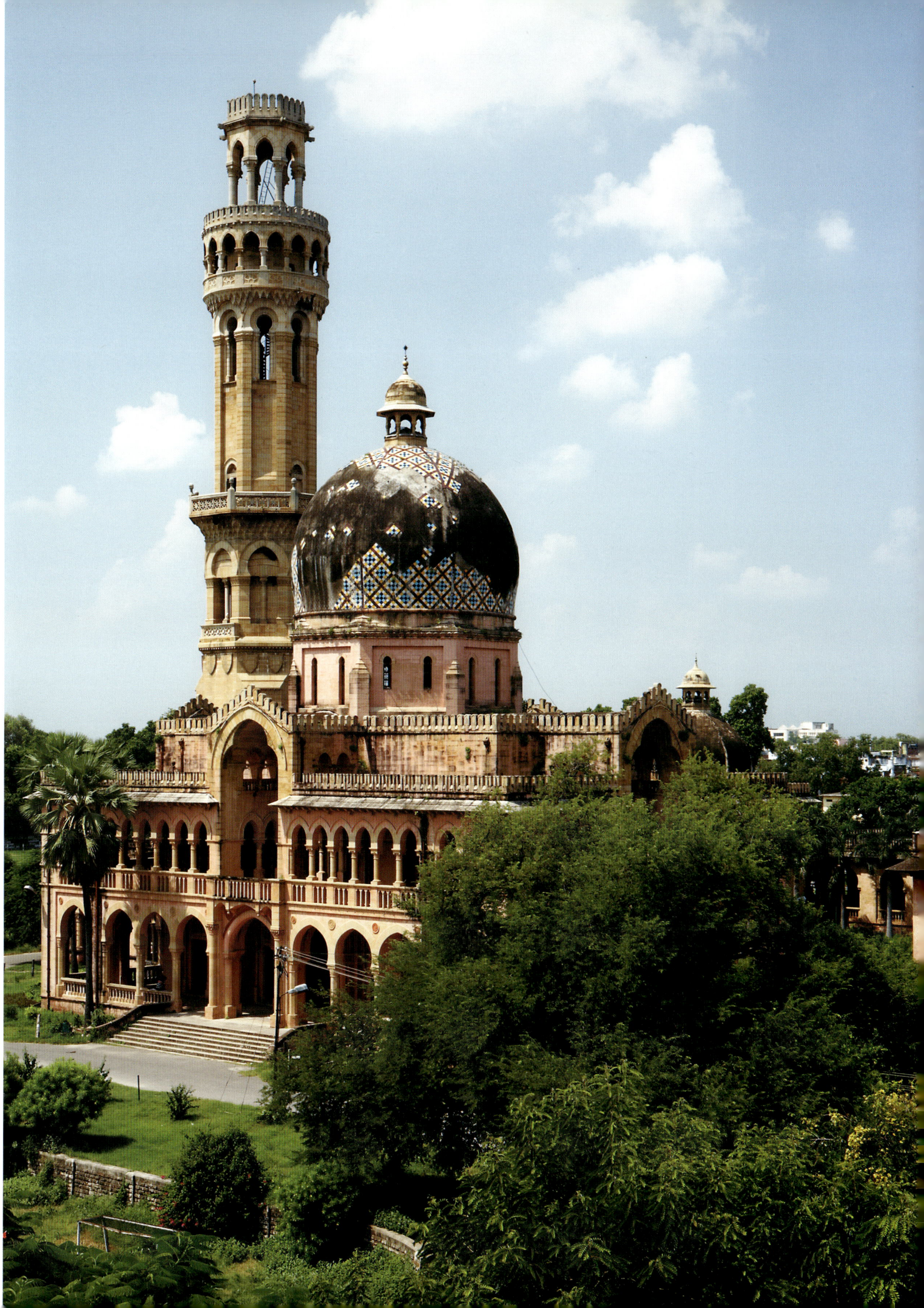

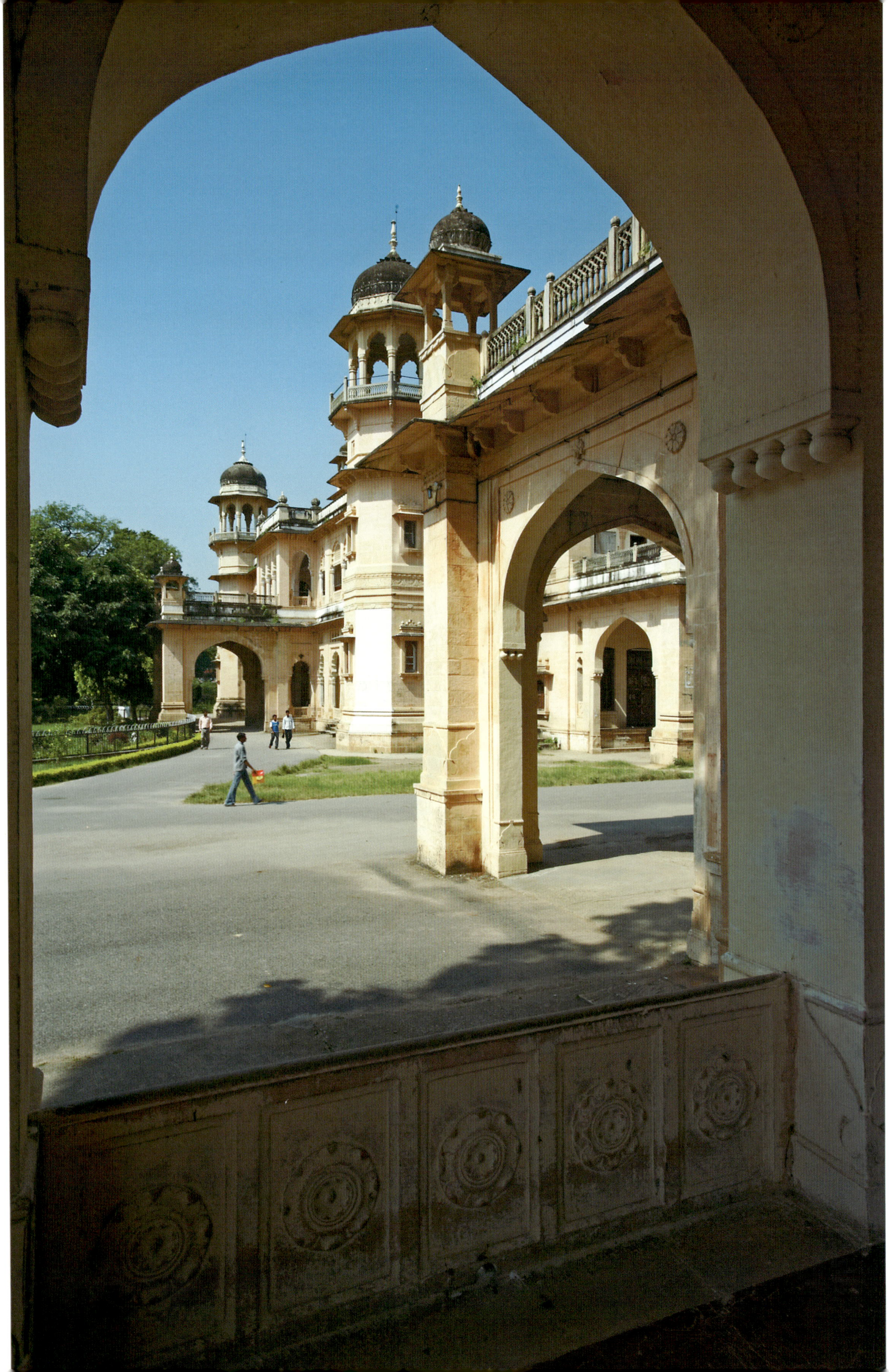

in the floral designs of capitols above stone pillars. A third vice-chancellor had these shelves cannibalized to make smaller shelves for a new science library. Some sort of restoration and preservation exercise is lately underway; however one is left wondering who will protect the heritage structures from authorized vandals.

Legends

My aesthetic researches into the University's trees and architecture were accompanied by my awed discovery of personalities on the campus. I heard of a professor who haggled over the price of tomatoes and saved every paisa he could, to gift it all away to science. One of his research students counted 63 patches on his overcoat. Yet when he went abroad to lecture and represent his country, he dressed immaculately. Another professor, every winter, would put a stack of blankets on the back-seat of his car and drive around on bitterly cold nights, to wrap them round homeless beggars shivering on roadside pavements. Three professors, from the departments of English, Sanskrit, and Physics, dialoguing over their afternoon tea, identified the location of what later would become the excavation site of the millennia-old buried township of Kaushambi. A professor of Chemistry, after retirement, became a recluse, and worked day and night to complete eight books on occult wisdom. An English professor, nearing 80, travelled back all the way from England because a former servant needed help. When a rushing undergraduate inadvertently bumped into the portly figure of a renowned professor at a bend and began blushing and apologizing profusely, the Don reassured him, "Not at all, Sir. It is entirely my pleasure, Sir. Do it again, Sir." When another undergraduate, not quite sure where to use the article in English, asked a professor, "Please, Sir, what is time?" the professor, delighted with the profundity of the question, sat him down beside him, launched into a long soliloquy on time and space, and concluded by offering him tea, standing up to shake his hand, and saying, "I am so glad, so very, very glad that the two of us could discuss such an abstruse topic for over two hours."

The story of the human presence in the University is a gestalt of many stories. It certainly would include the story of her distinguished teachers who were great scientists like Meghnad Saha, Nil Ratan Dhar, and K.S. Krishnan; creative writers like Firaq, Bachchan, Dharamvir Bharati, and Ram Kumar Verma; historians like Rushbrook Williams, Shafaat Ahmad Khan, R.P. Tripathi, and Tarachand; Indologists like Ganganatha Jha, Khetresh Chattopadhyaya, and Govind Chand Pande; mathematicians like Homersham Cox, A.C. Banerji, and Gorakh Prasad; encyclopedic minds like Thibaut, S.C. Deb, and Beni Prasad; institution builders like Amaranatha Jha, Durganand Sinha, and G.R. Sharma; and perhaps above all else, gentle, incorruptible, authentic, low-profile, caring human beings

4 *opposite*
The southern block of the Senate House complex. Formerly the library, it now houses the offices of the University.

5
The Allahabad University crest, wrought in cast-iron, on the gates of the University. The design was conceived by J.G. Jennings, Principal of Muir Central College in the late 19th century, and drawn by Asit Kumar Haldar.

6
The marble plaque set in the wall beside the east entrance to the Senate Hall. The plaque commemorates the establishment of the University in 1887.

like Adityaram Bhattacharya, Mahadev Govind Ranade, P.S.V. Naidu, Julien Mitter, J.K. Mehta, I.K. Taimni, K.K. Mehrotra, R.N. Deb, A.B. Lal, and Mohan Lal. The gestalt could not ignore the doings of distinguished alumni who became great scientists, writers, thinkers, teachers, scholars, judges, lawyers, politicians, administrators, journalists, and even the President, Prime Minister, or Chief Justice of India. The human narrative, however, cannot stop there, but must go on to contain the story of neglected nameless nobodies, who came to the University in thousands to receive but little. It must talk of the young who, in the '60s and the '70s of the last century, formed slogan-shouting student mobs and went around the campus, smashing window panes, disrupting work in classrooms and offices, having the University shut down for months, getting examinations postponed and sessions delayed, over trivial nothings. The irrational passion of those mobs often made me wonder whether chaos and indiscipline were not the language of the inarticulate who knew no other way of attacking the superficial orderliness and complacence of a system they found absurd and irrelevant to their lives.

The British empire gave its universities magnificent buildings and grounds to impress a subject nation with a show of opulence and grandeur, and pretence of concern for its welfare and development. It did not give the universities worthy, visionary goals. It set them trivial tasks to perform: to produce men who would help them rule the country by attending to sundry matters as government servants. The rewards of the examination system and campus life sought to inculcate elitist values. The accent was on manners, decorum, and style, loyalty to the badge, unquestioning acceptance, good memory, and ability to reproduce the acceptable answers, not on doubt, questioning, inquiry, and the cultivation of that intellectual rigour and creative intuition which could solve the real problems of building a new society in the postcolonial period. For quite some time after Independence, the University of Allahabad continued to turn out a sizeable crop of bureaucrats every year, setting about

7
A segment of the Science Faculty buildings, Muir College.

8
View of the Muir College Hostel, now known as the Amaranatha Jha Hostel, famous grooming ground for Civil Service aspirants during the decades immediately following Independence.

the task efficiently with values that were trite but adequate for the purpose, in what was called its golden period. If in spite of the absence of a truly profound vision and philosophy of education, the University produced some first-rate creative minds, it was because of the presence of great teachers on the campus and their individual effort.

The explosion of school education after India became free in 1947 pushed ever-swelling waves of students into the universities. Educators were not thinking how to bring about a radical change to give birth to an altogether different society. They were tinkering with the existing system geared to reward the elite and to discard and forget the weaker, poorer, and disadvantaged. Like many of its counterparts, Allahabad University naturally entered an era of turmoil and lawlessness. Indiscipline in the student body reached its peak after the lifting of the Emergency. It took the form of defiant large-scale copying in examinations. If allowed to use unfair means students would take the examinations. If prevented, they would walk out, tearing answer sheets and shouting slogans. There was a vice-chancellor who stayed behind

Manas Mukul Das

police protection at his residence and did not visit his office for 18 months, allowing examinations to turn into a farce. It was then that the teachers of the University shook off their slumber, sunk their differences, and stood as one body to restore sanity. It was a period of intense community thinking on the right role of education, the kind of atmosphere a university should have, teacher-student relationship, democracy, and a whole lot of other subjects. However, when the immediate crisis was over and teachers did not feel the threat of facing insult in examination halls, they returned to their easy ways. Questioning and idealism survived in many dialoguing groups of teachers and students but for the majority cynicism took a heavy toll. The once-upon-a-time elite University of Allahabad struggled for years to be picked up and rescued from the debris of universities floundering under the pressure of numbers and paucity of funds. Fortunate in having had a series of effective and reforming vice-chancellors in the last few years, its efforts finally succeeded and it secured the status of a Central University. Today the University is flush with funds. But funds do not make a university. Vision and people do.

As I was entering the Arts Campus one day, a student of mine asked me, "What does it mean, Sir – 'Quot rami tot arbores'?" His question brought back memories of the day I was admitted to the University as an undergraduate. Fascinated, I too had looked at the University motto wrought into the cast-iron of the gate and wondered. I saw the surging waters of the two rivers on the bank of whose confluence stood a gigantic banyan tree, many roots hanging from its branches. "University of Allahabad" written in iron letters arched over the tree in a semicircle. Below, quaint words completed the circle – "Quot rami tot arbores". I had seen the motto on the gates and delicately carved in white marble on the two sides of the main entrance to the Senate Hall, approached from the East Portico. I enquired and found out that Professor J.G. Jennings, Principal of the Muir Central College in the late 19th century, had conceived the design of the crest and that Asit Haldar had drawn it.

Akshaya-vat, the mythical Tree of Immortal Wisdom, stands in the many-thousand-year-old township of Allahabad, at the confluence of sacred rivers. Jennings, who had loved India, surely thought of the University as a Tree of Wisdom drawing its sap from the waters of many cultures – Vedantic, Puranic, Buddhist, Islamic, and Modern Liberal Scientific – and passing on its wisdom to its alumni who are the roots hanging from its branches, each ready to become a tree: Quot rami tot arbores, which means "As many branches, that many trees."

NOTES

1   *King's Story*, 1951, p. 170, quoted in M.L. Bhargava, *Hundred Years of Allahabad University*, Ashish Publishing House, New Delhi, 1987.
2   Quoted in Amaranatha Jha, ed., *A History of Muir Central College, 1872–1922*, Allahabad University, Allahabad, Chapter 1, "The Foundations".

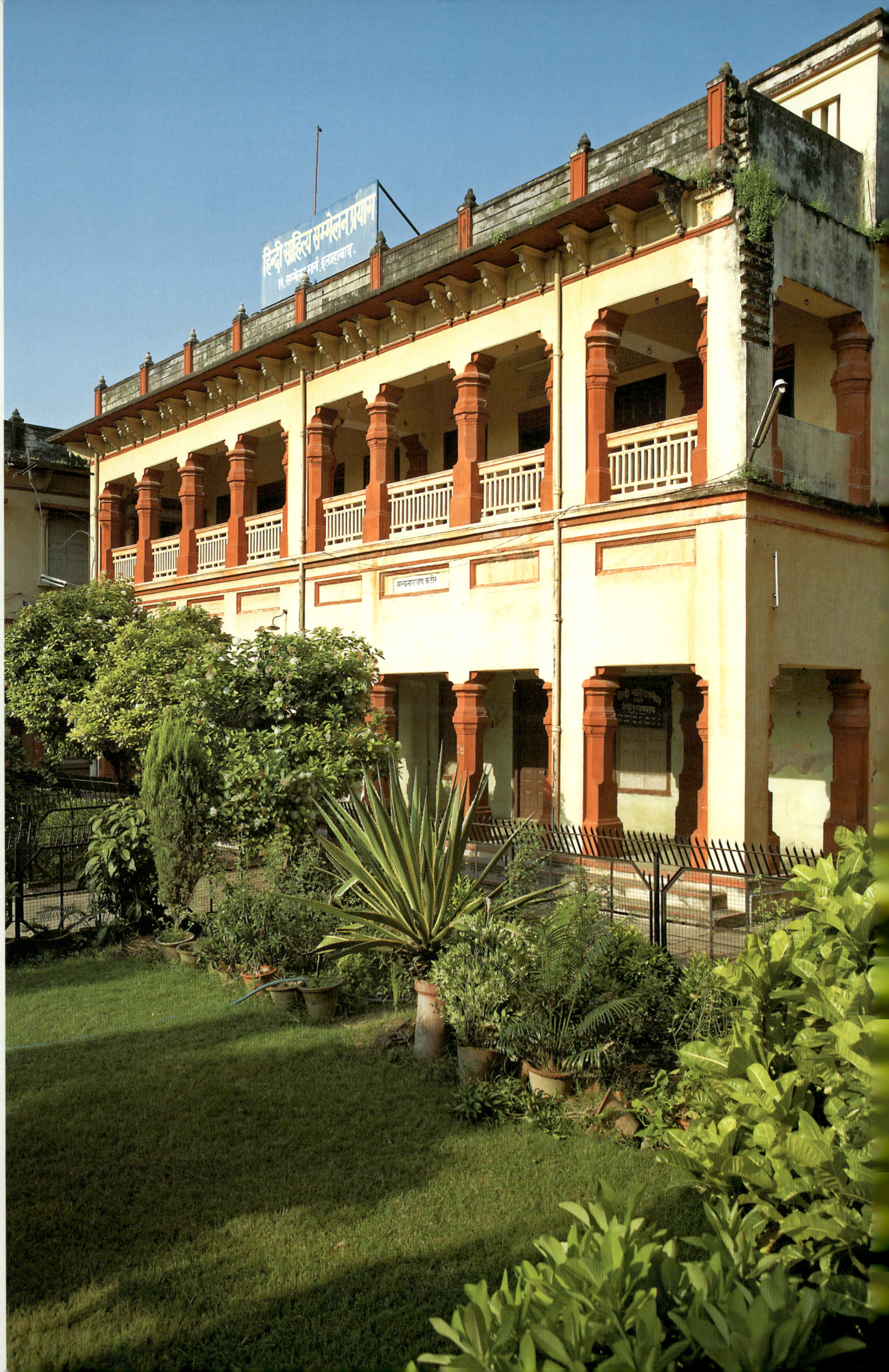
हिन्दी साहित्य सम्मेलन, प्रयाग

Prayagvad in Hindi Writing

Harish Trivedi

For almost the whole of the 20th century, Allahabad was the great centre of Hindi literature, its very *garh* – citadel or stronghold. Even now, when the glory has largely departed, the very name of the city evokes a golden afterglow in the hearts of all Hindi-lovers. There have, of course, been other centres of Hindi with their own different characteristics and contribution, but none of them has dominated and defined the whole landscape of Hindi and represented its very essence in the way Allahabad did through four or five successive phases and generations. Krishna Baldev Vaid (b. 1927), a major contemporary novelist who has never had much to do with Allahabad, once wrote of *Hindi Sahitya mein Prayagvad*, i.e. Allahabadism in Hindi Literature – and he seems to have got it just right.

Early Modernity
Such pre-eminence for Allahabad began towards the end of the 19th century, shortly after the death of Bharatendu Harishchandra (1850–85) of Banaras. The first forthright harbinger of the modern age in Hindi was probably Shridhar Pathak (1859–1928), who studied for two years in Muir Central College (which later became the University of Allahabad), and perhaps had better English than most Hindi writers of his generation. He wrote nature poetry of a Western romantic kind in Khari Boli as well as patriotic poems, and resigned his senior government post in 1914 after a tiff with his British superior in Simla. He then spent his retirement in Allahabad in a bungalow he built for himself in the new middle-class neighbourhood Lukergunj, where he devoted his time to literary pursuits and where he regularly hosted younger poets like Sumitranandan Pant, whom he sent his splendid horse-driven carriage to fetch and carry back. Though dilapidated, "Padamkot" still stands.

So do the buildings of the Indian Press, a short walk away from the University and diagonally across the grandly laid out gardens, originally called the Company Bagh (after the East India Company), then Alfred Park (after Prince Alfred, Duke of Edinburgh, who visited Allahabad), and now Chandra Shekhar Azad Park (after the revolutionary patriot who died in 1931 at age 25 in a police ambush at a fringe of the Park, just across the road from both the Muir Central College and the Hindu Hostel.) The Indian Press, unlike the Naval Kishore Press in Lucknow which published mainly in Urdu, published in the new rising languages, Hindi and English, and though the great battle to get Hindi recognized as an alternative to artificially propped-up Urdu was begun and won in Banaras by the Nagari Pracharini Sabha (established 1893), it was the Indian Press which later helped as much as any public agency in consolidating the new power of Hindi.

1 *opposite*
The Hindi Sahitya Sammelan building.

2
Shridhar Pathak, the first poet to use Khari Boli with success in modern Hindi poetry, bringing a new flavour to it. Courtesy Allahabad Museum.

One of the major ways in which it did so was by publishing from 1900 on, for the Nagari Pracharini Sabha, its monthly journal *Saraswati*, devoted to not only literature but a wider modern discourse. Its magisterial editor from 1903 to 1920 was Mahavir Prasad Dwivedi (1864–1938) who, as a peremptorily proactive editor, brought about a sea-change in the language of literary Hindi by consolidating and refining Khari Boli as the new medium of Hindi prose and verse alike. As the major vehicle of literary and intellectual modernity in Hindi, *Saraswati* was largely responsible for Hindi *navajagaran* or renaissance.

The Great Flowering: Chhayavad

In Dwivedi's time, the new Hindi poetry still seemed stilted, unmusical, and indeed prosaic. But this changed radically with the rise of the Chhayavadi (i.e., romantic-mystical) poets, who were to give Allahabad its distinct and supreme literary identity. Chhayavad is commonly seen as representing the second golden age of Hindi poetry, after the four great bhakti poets of the 15th–16th centuries – Kabir, Surdas, Mira, and Tulsidas. Of Chhayavad's own quartet of great poets, three lived in and breathed the air of Allahabad – Suryakanta Tripathi "Nirala" (1899–1961), Sumitranandan Pant (1900–77), and Mahadevi Varma (1907–87). Collectively, they brought to Allahabad a literary lustre which will remain its chief glory.

Pant, initially the most thrilling and polemically original of the three, had come from the lovely Himalayan village of Kausani to study at the University of Allahabad (which had been founded in 1887 and was the fifth-oldest university in India, after Bombay, Calcutta, and Madras, all founded in 1857, and Punjab at Lahore, founded in 1882); he withdrew without a degree in 1921 inspired by the Gandhian Non-Cooperation Movement. Mahadevi Varma, mismatched in a child marriage at the age of nine, which she boldly turned her back

3
An early number of the iconic journal *Saraswati*. Courtesy Hindustani Academy.

4
Saraswati served as a prestigious literary platform for many legendary Hindi writers. Courtesy Hindustani Academy.

on three years later, went to the Crosthwaite School in Allahabad and then to the University where she got an MA degree. She then taught at the Prayag Mahila Vidyapeeth, a nationalist institution for women, of which she was a long-serving principal; altogether, she lived her whole purposive life cheerfully following high Gandhian ideals.

In contrast, Nirala, who was brought up in Bengal, began his literary career in Calcutta and then lived for a while in Lucknow and in his village near Kanpur, before coming to Allahabad relatively late in his life. But he obviously found this laid-back easy-going city congenial to his own unconventional and unworldly lifestyle. The remote neighbourhood of Daragunj, on the Ganga, still reverberates to legendary tales of his carefree, penurious, and yet generous ways which it would be a cultural travesty to call bohemian. He is now regarded as probably the greatest Hindi poet of the 20th century, and a remarkably lifelike statue of this radical original poet, who never went to university, now stands in front of the University Library.

Nirala, Pant, and Mahadevi were widely different from each other in their personalities and chosen trajectories of life, and yet they were for decades bound to each other in a close and intricate web of poetry and proximity. Never have three poets of such outstanding stature inhabited the same city at the same time in the whole history of Hindi literature. The abiding literary mystique of Allahabad owes more to the conjunction and confluence of this great trinity than to anything else.

Prateek, Parimal, and the Progressives

Pant lived on till 1977 and Mahadevi till a decade later, gracing and inspiring the Hindi public sphere in Allahabad and beyond.

Both won the Jnanpith Award and achieved a literary eminence that no Hindi poet since then has matched. But Nirala, the greatest of them all, had already died in 1961, after a few years of mental instability during which he would often deliver impassioned interrogative monologues, mostly in English, addressed to another rather different son of Allahabad, the anglicized Jawaharlal Nehru. Mahadevi, though continuing as an educationist, prose writer, and translator from Sanskrit, had stopped writing poetry altogether in 1942, apparently reproached into silence by a piece of advice from an elder poet that the voice of Mother India should also be heard in her poetry, which had always been characterized by an intense transcendental mysticism. Pant remained productive for the longest, but he had travelled in the opposite direction, through Gandhism and Marxism to another kind of mysticism inspired partly by Sri Aurobindo. Anyhow, Chhayavad had already done its great work, by proving to even the most sceptical of readers that modern Hindi

5 and 6
Script of a poem in Nirala's handwriting, and a portrait of the poet. Courtesy Allahabad Museum.

Prayagvad in Hindi Writing

7 and 8
Mahadevi Varma, and a page of one of her manuscripts. Courtesy Allahabad Museum.

9 and 10
Sumitranandan Pant, and the Jnanpith Award he received in 1968. Courtesy Allahabad Museum.

poetry in its new medium of Khari Boli could be as expressive, musical, and popular as any poetry before.

In any case, already in the 1940s, there were at work in Hindi two new literary impulses, generally identified as *prayogvad* (experimentalism or modernism) and *pragativad* (Marxist progressivism). They initially overlapped in some respects but quickly diverged so radically as to be each other's opposites and declared adversaries. In this embattled scenario, Allahabad again turned out to be the *dharmakshetra/kurukshetra*, or the appropriate arena, where much of the action took place.

The founding figure of literary modernism in Hindi was Sachchidanand Hiranand Vatsyayan "Ajneya" (1911–87), a peripatetic man by temperament who, however, came and made Allahabad his home in 1946. It was here that he gathered a group of talented young Hindi writers around himself, inspired them with his own dedication and vision, and brought out a journal of new writing *Prateek* (symbol), which has been compared with *Saraswati* for its pioneering initiative and influence (though not its reach and longevity). Indeed, Ajneya and these other writers formed a kind of modernist commune (if that is not too flagrant a contradiction in terms), for they stayed together in a large bungalow at 14 Hastings Road, where the hall in the middle was the office of *Prateek* while the four bedroom suites around it were occupied by Sripat Rai, Nemichandra Jain, Bharat Bhushan Agarwal, and Ajneya himself, with their families. (Earlier, Sumitranandan Pant too had shared a house on Beli Road with the younger poet Bachchan; it still stands with its nameplate "Basudha", in which "ba" stood for Bachchan, "su" for Sumitranandan and "dha" for *dham*, i.e. abode.)

Ajneya's experiment in common living and common writing was too idealistic to last and in 1949 he was obliged to close down the journal and move on to Delhi. But these years were so intense and productive a phase of his life that a biographer of his has characterized them in a chapter-title as "The High Tide of Creativity" as well as "Pilgrimage to Prayag". The episode represents the great pull that Allahabad had already begun to exercise on all kinds of Hindi writers from wherever to come and make it their home.

11
The courtyard of the house where Harivansh Rai Bachchan lived in the early years. The locked door opens into the room in which his famous poem *Madhushala* was written.

12
Indian Posts' first-day-cover commemorating Harivansh Rai Bachchan. Courtesy H.S. Saxena.

Also in the 1940s, a literary organization was founded by a few young students who felt oppressed by the highly anglophone and Westernized ambience of the University, especially prevalent in snobbish organizations such as the Friday Club and the Foundation Club, and who wanted anyhow to set up a literary club for Hindi. This was Parimal, which began life at an informal meeting on December 10, 1944, and which came to be identified with the very spirit of Allahabad as time went on. A major all-India conference of writers not only from Hindi but also from other languages (such as Tarashankar Banerjee, Shivaram Karanth, and B.K. Bhattacharya) that it hosted from May 3 to 5, 1957, on the theme "The Writer and State Patronage", became a historical landmark. Moreover, it seems to have provoked the Pragatisheel Lekhak Sangh (the Progressive Writers' Association) to hold a major conference of its own later the same year, December 15–17, on the theme "Free India and the Writer" – once again of course at Allahabad.

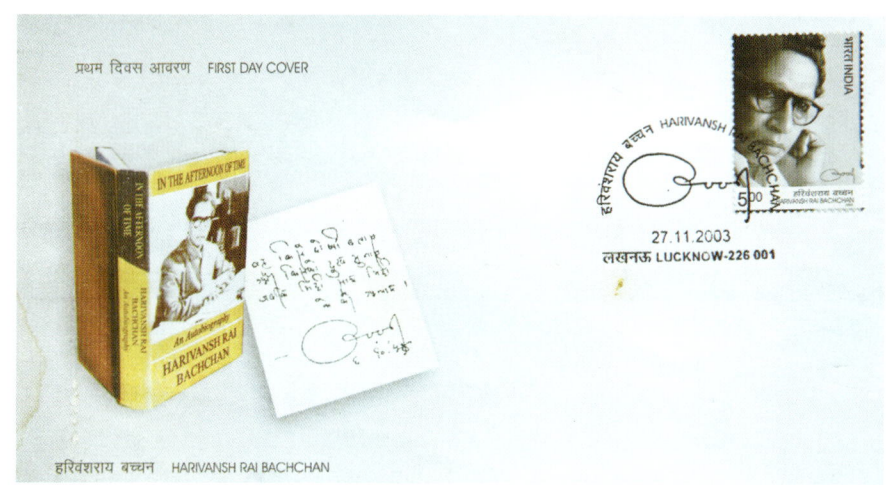

Parimal went on as a close-knit group of literary friends who met regularly to read their fresh works to each other or to debate literary and cultural issues, and in its own eyes, it remained a congenial, good-humoured, and liberal club without any explicit ideology. But it was seen by others as having played a nefarious (or, alternatively, commendable) role in thwarting the spread

Prayagvad in Hindi Writing

13
Bharti Bhavan Library in Chowk Gangadas. The Library was an important centre in the world of Hindi letters, even supplying books ordered by eminent freedom-fighters housed in Naini Jail. Courtesy John Harrison.

of ideologically committed writing in Hindi. The progressives had no one city as their centre, but the non-progressives were all believed, right from the days of "escapist" Chhayavad, to have congregated in Allahabad. In fact, in his magnum opus *Terhe Merhe Raste* (1946; Zig-zag Ways), the novelist Bhagwati Charan Varma had already staged a long scene set in 1930 in which an Indian communist, who has been educated and indoctrinated in Germany, comes to Allahabad to spread the Marxist message, and meets at a big tea-party all the notable Hindi writers living in the city. (From Nirala, Pant, and Mahadevi to about a dozen others, they are all represented here in this fictional scene in very thin disguises and with rollicking comedy.) In the end, the radical proselytizer is told in no uncertain terms by a young writer (who is obviously a self-portrait by Varma): "So you wish to use us writers as propagandists for Russia and its socialism? Mister Umanath, you are mistaken, for we writers are not going to be beguiled by you."

Arrivals and Departures
Bhagwati Charan Varma was educated at the University of Allahabad and had already written a novel, *Teen Varsh* (1936), which has for its hero a brilliant student of the University who grew up as a poor orphan but now falls in love with a classmate who is the daughter of Sir Krishna Kumar, the leading lawyer of Allahabad. When she refuses to marry him, he goes away and slips into a vortex of moral degeneration but returns on the last page to shame her for her materialistic heartlessness.

Such a hero is a familiar figure in the Hindi fiction of the time, with the mismatch between meritorious academic excellence and social and economic handicaps providing a poignant theme. But this basic plot was transformed into something transcendental by Dharamvir Bharati (1925–91) in his novel *Gunahon ka Devata* (1959), a highly lyrical and emotional narrative in which the bright boy and his university teacher's daughter do not name their love for each other even to themselves while they painfully struggle to sublimate it out of existence. Despite its self-confessed "immaturity", this is in many ways the quintessential Allahabad novel, copies of which were for decades passed around from room to room in the hostels of Allahabad University while undergraduates went around quoting whole paragraphs from it and identifying with its intensely romantic-idealist vision. It is also a bit of what may be called a Nehruvian novel, for it has well-developed Muslim and Christian characters too who bring their own culturally embedded perspectives to bear on the theme of love and marriage.

Bharati was born in Allahabad in an old *mohalla* named Atarsuiya (the name deriving, it is claimed, from Atri-Anusuya who had their ashram there in ancient times), and his other less romantic fiction offers an unflinchingly realistic depiction of the struggles of that mode of indigent life. Another major writer who was born on "the wrong side of the railway line" (in E.M. Forster's acute phrase) was Harivansh Rai Bachchan (1907–2003), whose *Madhushala* (1935) remains by far the best-selling volume of modern Hindi poetry. His evocation of old half-rural Allahabad, and especially of his own *mohalla* called Chak, in his four-volume autobiography, is one of the most culturally intimate evocations in Hindi of our pre-Westernized lives in the early decades of the 20th century.

It is sometimes pointed out that besides Bachchan and Bharati, hardly any Hindi writer of note who is identified with Allahabad was actually born there. (And as it happened, both left for bigger cities, Bombay and Delhi!) But given the astounding number of major and minor writers who have arrived in a constant stream over the decades to make Allahabad their home, this only attests to the magnetic and almost mythic attraction of the city. Perhaps the most remarkable of these writers is Gyanranjan (b. 1936), who was educated at the University of Allahabad but could find a job only a fair distance away in Jabalpur. Nevertheless, he has kept coming back to Allahabad compulsively all his life as often and for as long as possible. In common critical regard, he has written many of the finest Hindi short stories of the last half-century, some of which are set in Allahabad (e.g. *Amrood ka Ped* – The Guava Tree), some which evoke Allahabad indirectly but unmistakably (e.g. *Manhoos Bangla* – The Wretched Bungalow), and at least one that even seems to depict, with phantasmagoric intensity, his own obsession with Allahabad (*Anubhav* – Experience). In being a waif, he is a truer son of the city than most who have lived there.

The Hindi literary world of 21st-century Allahabad continues to buzz, with an enterprising new generation of poets, translators, and fiction writers of merit carrying on the tradition, albeit on an altered scale.

بسم الله الرحمن الرحیم
مکتوب از جانب سلطان عالم محمد دارا شکوه انار الله برهانه بحضرت
فانی فی الله شیخ محب الله الٰه آبادی قدس سره
قل الله ثم ذرهم
جواب از جانب عارف بالله شیخ محب الله قدس سره بشاهزاده
سلطان عالم محمد دارا شکوه نور الله مرقده

Urdu and Persian Literature

Shamsur Rahman Faruqi

Ai abe raude Ganga vo din hain yad tujhko/utra tere kinare jab karvan hamara
(O mighty Ganga! do you recall that day when we travellers stopped on your banks)
– Mohammed Iqbal

In the year 1778, a young man called Amiruddin Ahmad left his home in Ilahabad (Allahabad) and set out for Azimabad (Patna), Murshidabad, and finally Calcutta (Kolkata). His purpose was to meet with and gather accounts of poets with the view of writing a *tazkira* (Biographical Dictionary of Poets). His main motivation for compiling the Dictionary was his interest in Urdu and Persian poetry, and also, as he said later, to provide a corrective to some of the opinions expressed by the great Delhi poet Mir Muhammad Taqi Mir (1722–1810) who, in his own Dictionary (which was, in 1752, the first ever of Urdu poets) had some nasty things to say about many well-known poets of Delhi.

Having been born around 1756, Amiruddin Ahmad, or Abul Hasan Amrullah Ilahabadi, as he later called himself, was barely 22 when he went out into the world to collect material for his book. He is also known to have been in Banaras (Varanasi), Ghazipur, Farrukhabad, and Lakhnau (Lucknow), the last in 1780, and in company with his older brother and tutor, Maulvi Khairuddin Ilahabadi, a well-known scholar and poet of his time. Abul Hasan began writing his Biographical Dictionary in about 1779. He kept adding to it from time to time, finishing it in 1781. Called *Tazkira-e Masarrat Afza* (Delight Enhancing Biographical Dictionary of Poets), the work won instant popularity, but its manuscripts became extremely scarce over time and now only two copies are known to be extant. It was printed for the first time in 1955–56 in a magazine by the great scholar Qazi Abdul Wadud (1896–1984) and has since been an important source of information and anecdotes about Urdu and Persian poets of Allahabad, Azimabad, Calcutta, and Delhi, and many smaller towns.

I devote so much space to Abul Hasan to show that Allahabadi writers and intellectuals in the 18th century were not just imitators of Delhi; they evince a spirit of inquiry and independent thought and preferred to gather information on their own, and make their own decisions. This will become more apparent as our narrative progresses.

The origins of Indo-Islamic literary culture in Allahabad may be traced to Shah Muhibbullah Ilahabadi (1587–1648) who wrote copiously in Persian and Arabic on abstruse Sufi subjects. He was a close follower of the great Andalusian Sufi mystic and poet Muhyiuddin Ibn-e Arabi (1165–1240), popularly known as Shaikh-e Akbar (the greatest

1 *opposite*
Record of correspondence between Shah Muhibbullah Ilahabadi and Dara Shikoh in the 17th century.

master). Shah Muhibbullah himself was therefore always referred to as Shaikh-e Kabir (the great master). Ibn-e Arabi's teaching was based on the idea of *wahdat-ul wajud* (the unity of beings) and his pronouncements have sometimes caused discomfort to literalist or orthodox believers. The Mughal Prince Dara Shikoh (1615–59) was an admirer of Shah Muhibbullah's. He once sent Shah Muhibbullah a questionnaire on esoteric Sufi matters to which the Shaikh replied in great detail. Both the letters are preserved in the extant voluminous correspondence of Shah Muhibbullah.

Aurangzeb, perhaps suspicious of the doctrine of *wahdat-ul wajud* as propounded by Shah Muhibbullah in one of his celebrated works called *Taswiyah* (Equalization), and also unhappy with the late Shaikh's friendliness toward Dara Shikoh, once summoned Syed Muhammad Qannauji, one of his courtiers and also a disciple of Shah Muhibbullah. The story goes that Aurangzeb commanded Qannauji to explain and interpret some of the Shaikh's statements so as to be in agreement with the tenets of the *sharia* (Islamic religious law), stipulating that if he failed to do so, he should publicly burn his Shaikh's tract. Syed Muhammad Qannauji reportedly answered that his Shaikh had written those words after attaining a certain spiritual status which was too far above his own present state. Once he reached the station of the Shaikh, he said, he would satisfactorily explain and interpret the words of his Master. As for burning the work, Qannauji is reported to have said, there was plenty of fire in the Emperor's kitchen and there was no need to use a poor man's fire for the purpose. At this, Aurangzeb dropped the matter, though some ulema declared that Shah Muhibbullah, by virtue of his questionable views about appearance and reality, did not deserve to be called a Muslim.

Allahabad's other great centre for Sufi thought and Persian (and later also Urdu) literature was founded by Shaikh Muhammad Afzal (1628–1712/1714). Apart from writing prolifically in Persian and Arabic on esoteric as well as pedagogic subjects, Shah (the honorifics "Shah" and "Shaikh" are interchangeable; the Sufi culture in Allahabad and many eastern districts prefers "Shah") Muhammad Afzal was a proficient poet in Persian. While Shah Muhibbullah Ilahabadi and his followers were viewed with some hostility among a section of the people, Shah Muhammad Afzal seems to have enjoyed universal esteem, not excluding Aurangzeb himself on whose orders the *subahdar* of Ilahabad constructed a beautiful mosque in 1677 for the use of the Shaikh and his followers and visitors. In 1681, again at the Emperor's command, the *subahdar* built the Shaikh's dwelling place (hospice, or *khanqah* in technical parlance). Both mosque and *khanqah* exist and are in use to this day.

Shah Muhammad Yahya (there is a neighbourhood extant in Allahabad called Yahyagunj after him) is better known as Shah Khubullah. Born in 1660, he was a nephew of Shaikh Muhammad Afzal and succeeded his uncle at the *khanqah*. He died in 1731. He was a good poet in Persian, but his eminence as a man of letters was eclipsed by his second son, Shah Muhammad Fakhir Zair (1708–50). Zair's poetry commanded much prestige for being in the mode of Sa'di (1184–1291) and Hafiz (1325?–98), the two greatest Iranian ghazal poets. His rubais also are well-known. Shah Khubullah's eldest son Shah Muhammad Tahir (1698–1721) was primarily a scholar who also wrote poetry. Another of Shah Khubullah's sons Shah

Muhammad Nasir Afzali (1710–50) was a major Persian poet and was often described as a "second Nasir Ali" (Nasir Ali Sirhindi, d. 1696, is widely regarded as a Persian poet who took the "Indian style" of Persian poetry to new heights).

Shaikh Ali Hazin (1691–1766), an Iranian nobleman and distinguished poet, sought refuge in India in 1733 after the Afghans seized power in Iran. Umdat-ul Mulk Amir Khan Anjam (d. 1747), courtier, administrator, diplomat, musicologist, poet, patron of poets, and a highly placed nobleman at Emperor Muhammad Shah's court, patronized Ali Hazin and was instrumental in getting him immense financial benefits from the Emperor. Unfortunately, Ali Hazin was not a person suited to accept favours with grace. He was vitriolic against India and Indians and was particularly disdainful of Indian Persian poets. During his *subahdari* of Allahabad, Umdat-ul Mulk promoted the arts and letters there and befriended Muhammad Afzal Sabit (d. 1737), a man of great learning and a distinguished poet. Sabit and his son Muhammad Azim Sabat (1700–48), also a poet, moved to Delhi along with Umdat-ul Mulk and took their place among the poets of Delhi. Shaikh Ali Hazin once made some severely censorious remarks about a verse of Sabit's and also alleged that Sabit had plagiarized the theme of his verse from an older Iranian poet. Word promptly got round to Sabit who said that Hazin was a plagiarist himself. Sabit then produced within four days a tract in which he quoted 500 verses of Ali Hazin and an equal number of verses from older poets and stated that all these verses of Ali Hazin were in fact plagiarisms of the earlier ones. According to a contemporary Iranian chronicler, "Thus did Sabit reduce to trash five hundred verses of Hazin within a very few days."

The 18th century witnessed great artistic and cultural achievement in India. It was also a century in which the creativity of Indian Persian poets and scholars grew to full maturity and boundless self-assurance. Shaikh Ali Hazin's advent occasioned a long-running debate about the competence of Indians in Persian and it fell to Sabit,

2
Interior of the mosque of Shah Muhibbullah known as the Daira-e Sheikh Muhibbullah Shah.

an Ilahabadi, to make the first important contribution to this debate. Literary activity in Allahabad luckily gained an auspicious participant in the person of Emperor Shah Alam II (r. 1759–1806) who himself stayed in Allahabad from about 1765 to January 1771. Shah Alam knew many languages, including Sanskrit and Arabic. He wrote poetry and prose in Hindi, Persian, and Braj Bhasha, and, according to a contemporary chronicler, wrote poetry in Sanskrit too. He favoured Hindi (as Urdu was then called) over Persian for everyday conversation.

An important cultural development in the 18th century was the adoption, and then assumption of leadership, of Rekhta/Hindi poetry by the poets of Delhi in preference to, or alongside, Persian. Almost all of these poets were born between 1685 and 1725 and their influence spread far into the land, including the south and the east. Allahabad could not remain untouched by the new literary wave and Urdu poetry in Allahabad may be said properly to begin with Shah Ghulam Qutbuddin Musib (1726–73). He was the son of Shah Muhammad Fakhir Zair and was married to Abul Hasan's sister. He is generally regarded as more eminent than his father because in addition to his being a Sufi master and scholar, he wrote poetry in Arabic, Persian, and Rekhta/Hindi and also spent much of his time travelling, ultimately dying in Mecca.

Shah Muhammad Nasir Afzali's son Shah Muhammad Ajmal (1747–1820) was a distinguished poet and author in Persian and Arabic who also occasionally wrote Urdu poetry. One of his chief distinctions is that he made a Persian translation of the *Quran* – the third known Persian translation of the holy book made in India. While his disciples and followers must have benefited by the translation, it however has remained unpublished.

Shah Muhammad Ajmal and his nephew Shah Ghulam Azam Afzal (1810–58) were friends with Imam Bakhsh Nasikh (1776–1838) the great Lakhnavi master of Urdu poetry and almost the founder of an entirely new style of ghazal. Nasikh was a frequent house guest at the *khanqah* of Shah Muhammad Ajmal (which later came to be

3
The gateway to the Daira-e Shah Ajmal.

known as Daira-e Shah Ajmal). It was here that Nasikh composed his famous verse:

> Three flowing at Tribeni, two from my eyes;
> Now Ilahabad too is Panjab!

Nasikh formally accepted Shah Ghulam Azam Afzal as his pupil. One of Shah Ghulam Azam Afzal's pupils was the great Sufi poet Abdul Alim Asi Sikandarpuri (1834–1917) who has the distinction of being a Sufi poet in Nasikh's style: witty, somewhat sardonic, and also studded with far-fetched verbal conceits. It was a style generally considered unsuitable for Sufi themes.

The story so far of the growth of Urdu and Persian literary culture has been almost entirely the story of one House: that of Shah Muhammad Afzal. This was to change in the 19th century, but Abul Hasan's chronicle gives us information about many other poets active in 18th-century Allahabad as well. One of them was Sarb Sukh Divanah (1727?–88/89) who was a legendary figure of his times as the model of Indo-Muslim culture. Abul Hasan gives us a rare nugget of information about him to the effect that Nawab Shuja-ud-daulah appointed him Mir-e Bahri (Admiral of the River Fleet) at Allahabad and that Divanah didn't mix much with the locals. Among many other poets of Allahabad, both Hindu and Muslim, whom Abul Hasan mentions, noteworthy are Shah Ghulam Yahya Insaf (d. 1780) who wrote delightful comic verse in Urdu and is perhaps the first

4
Verandah of Akbar Ilahabadi's home, now a school.

URDU AND PERSIAN LITERATURE

5 and 6
Portrait of Munshi Premchand, and a page of his diary showing random jottings, some significant. Courtesy Allahabad Museum.

Urdu poet to devote himself exclusively to comic verse, and Shah Muhammad Alim Betab (d. 1791), a maternal grandson of Shah Muhammad Yahya. He wrote in both Persian and Urdu. Among his pupils was Kanji Sahai Mateen who commanded a good reputation as a Persian poet in the early 19th century.

Mirza Kalb-e Husain Khan Nadir, a middle-grade officer in the service of the Company, composed in 1831 *Tazkira-e Shaukat-e Nadiri* (Biographical Dictionary: Nadir's Magnificence) about the poets active in Allahabad. He tells us that there are at least 100 full-time poets in Allahabad at the time of his writing. He records 70 poets in his dictionary of which a full dozen are Hindu. Nadir says that Urdu poetry is now not so prominent in the cultural life of the city as it was in the time of Shah Muhammad Alim; even so, "some of us organize regular mushairas. Apart from the locals, many of the 42 non-local poets who are resident here also take part in them."

Interestingly, Nadir's little tract has an Introduction which is rather too long for a book of its size. Yet for us today it is extremely valuable because it is full of information about the contemporary literary and social culture of Allahabad. For instance, Nadir tells the reader that the proper way to recite poetry in an assembly is to enunciate the words clearly; your voice should be fully audible to those present; you should not recite your poems in a singing tone of voice. Nadir strongly disapproves of poets who make dramatic gestures and use "a special tone of voice" while reciting poetry. We should perhaps extrapolate Nadir's remarks generally to poets of that time, and not to just those of Allahabad.

Towards the end of the 19th century, the House of Shah Muhammad Afzal ceased to occupy centre stage in the literary culture of Allahabad. Two major players at that time were Ghulam Imam Shaheed (d. 1879) and Ghulam Ghaus Bekhabar (1824–1905). Both were men of substance in society and both wrote extremely good poetry and prose in Persian. Bekhabar is also known for his friendship with Ghalib.

After a hiatus of more than two centuries, the House of Shah Muhibbullah Ilahabadi re-entered the literary scene in the person of Akbar Ilahabadi (1846–1921), one of whose sisters was married to Syed Sahib Ali, a direct descendant of Shah Muhibbullah. Akbar Ilahabadi was arguably the greatest Urdu poet of Allahabad. He was also Urdu's greatest political and social satirist. He was perhaps the first Indian to recognize that culture, big business, and politics went side by side in the colonial system of governance, and that modernization was actually a powerful weapon to establish and spread colonial power. Akbar was a passionate nationalist and wrote in a famous verse:

Were Akbar not the Government's concubine,

SHAMSUR RAHMAN FARUQI

> You would find him too among Gandhi's gopis.

He collected a series of his short poems under the title *Gandhi Namah* (Gandhi's Book) for whose epigraph he wrote another famous verse, as follows:

> The revolution is here:
> It's a new world, a new tumult,
> *The Book of Kings* is done;
> It's the age of *The Book of Gandhi* now.

Later critics chose to see his distrust and hatred of the colonial power's modernizing steps as a sign of his backwardness and blind conservatism, but our experience of globalization and the economic hegemony of the West in the 21st century vindicates Akbar as the first postcolonial poet.

Sir Syed Ahmad Khan (1817–98) was resident at Allahabad during his years of membership of the Legislative Council in the 1870s. The building now famous as Anand Bhavan was once owned by him. He continued to stay in Allahabad off and on even later. Syed Ahmad Khan's close friend Maulvi Nazir Ahmad (1831–1912), novelist, theologian, social reformer, jurisprudent, and much else besides, also lived in Allahabad during the 1870s. The founding of Muir Central College (1873), later to become the University of Allahabad, caused the arrival of some other major Urdu writers here from Delhi and elsewhere. Among them was the essayist, historian, mathematician, Maulvi Zakaullah (1832–1910). Later, there were Mahdi Hasan Nasiri (1885–1931) and the great historian Tara Chand (1888–1973). All of them taught Urdu at the Muir Central College at one time or other.

Akbar Ilahabadi and his teacher Vaheed Ilahabadi (1829–92) are also to be remembered as the last ghazal poets of Allahabad who wrote in the "classical" mode. By the time of Akbar's death, the influence of English on Urdu literature had all but superseded the prestige of the ghazal in the classical mode. Soon enough, new ideas about the social and revolutionary relevance of literature began to sweep the

7
Portrait of Firaq Gorakhpuri. Courtesy Allahabad Museum.

8
The Hindustani Academy building.

9
Pages from an antique *Quran* owned by the Daira-e Shah Ajmal.

board. Premchand (1880–1936), the great Urdu and Hindi writer, studied and worked in Allahabad for many years, off and on. He said that he never wrote a story unless the incident which he was narrating had some psychological or social truth. The Progressive Writers' Association (PWA) at its inception consisted mainly of Urdu writers, and Premchand delivered the Presidential address at its first convention in 1936 in Lucknow. Among other notable PWA writers who worked in Allahabad in the 1930s and '40s are PWA's founder Syed Sajjad Zaheer (1905–73) and Ahmad Ali (1910–84). Raghupati Sahai Firaq (1896–1982) was a Gorakhpuri by birth but spent nearly all his life in Allahabad. Poet, critic, fiction writer, translator, conversationalist, Firaq Gorakhpuri is widely regarded as one of the greatest Urdu men of letters. It is generally held that he revolutionized the Urdu ghazal, added new dimensions to the rubai, and wrote perhaps the best creative criticism in Urdu.

Premchand is rightly regarded as the greatest fiction writer in both Hindi and Urdu. Similar is the case of Upendra Nath Ashk (1910–96), an Urdu writer who settled in Allahabad after the Partition and then turned his vast talent to both Hindi and Urdu. Ashk was an informal Progressive, like Firaq, but by the 1950s Allahabad had become an extremely important locus of the PWA. The Progressive critic Professor Syed Aijaz Husain wrote *Nae Adabi Rujhanat* (New Trends in Literature) in 1947, perhaps the first full-length study of post-1936 literature in Urdu. Aijaz Husain influenced a host of notable writers who were his students at one time or other. Among them the greatest name is that of Syed Ehtesham Husain (1912–72), the chief ideologue of the Progressives. Then there were the scholar and critic Syed Vaqar Azim (1910–76), the critic Mujtaba Husain (1922–89), and the scholar, critic, and linguist Gian Chand Jain (1923–2007).

Urdu's literary culture in Allahabad was greatly enriched up to the early 1950s by the Hindustani Academy (established 1928) and its Urdu magazine *Hindustani*. Asghar Gondvi (1880–1936), a major Urdu poet of the time, was its editor. Premchand, the eminent linguist and scholar Abdus Sattar Siddiqi (1885–1972), and the eminent jurist and lover of Urdu Sir Tej Bahadur Sapru (1875–1949) were among the Academy's founding members. Hriday Nath Kunzru (1887–1978) who later became President of Anjuman Taraqqi-e Urdu (Hind), India's premier NGO in the field of Urdu letters, was among many in the circle of Tej Bahadur Sapru who were also lovers of Urdu. Other prominent Hindus like Amaranatha Jha, the famous professor of English, and lawyers Sir Sunder Lal, Gyanendra Kumar, N.P. Asthana, and Anand Narain Mulla, continued to love and live Urdu letters.

Urdu journalism in Allahabad can be said to have begun with Sada Sukh Lal who started his newspaper *Nurul Absar* (The Light of the Eyes) from Allahabad in 1852. By about 1900, there were at least seven Urdu newspapers being published from Allahabad. Like *Hindustani*, other Urdu literary magazines of Allahabad were catalysts as well as promoters of new writing from the early years of the 20th century. *Adeeb* was edited by Naubat Rai Nazar (1866–1923), Pyare Lal Shakir (1880–1956), and lastly by Haseer Azimabadi (1882–1922) during its short but influential life from 1910 to 1913. Syed Aijaz Husain edited *Karavan* (The Caravan) in the 1940s. In the '50s the monthly *Fasana* (Story) which published only short stories was a great success. Firaq Gorakhpuri and the economist Ram Pratap Bahadur were among its contributors. During the late '50s and early '60s Mahmud Ahmad Hunar's literary digest *Shahkar* (Masterpiece) printed some of the best modern Urdu literature from the subcontinent. The present writer's *Shabkhoon* (Surprise Attack by Night), in spite of its unusual name became the paradigmatic space for modernist writing and literary theory during its life of nearly 40 years (1966–2005).

NOTE

This text was first published online in September 2007 at <http://www.columbia.edu/itc/mealac/pritchett/00fwp/srf/txt_allahabad.html>

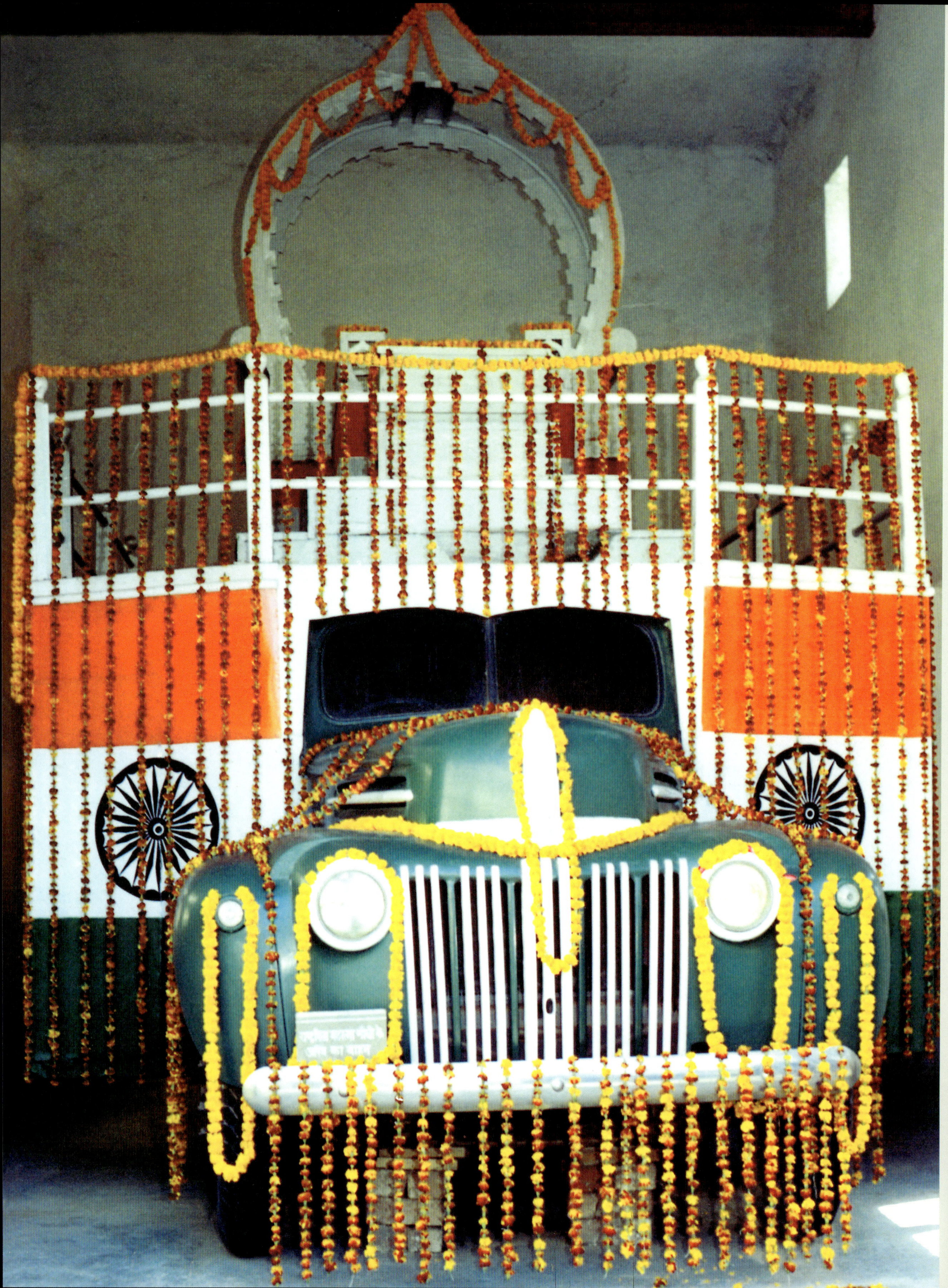

Nehru and Later

Gangeya Mukherji

Allahabad had enjoyed a fairly dominant position during the National Movement through its association with the Nehrus. Independence brought hardly any discernible change in the tenor of civic life in Allahabad when a popular government assumed the charge of directing the nation's affairs. The city could, and did with justifiable pride, claim that it had sent to Parliament in Delhi as its representatives men who led exemplary public lives. Both Jawaharlal Nehru and Lal Bahadur Shastri nourished their ties with Allahabad, but laid far greater stress on the larger issues before the country rather than allocating major government projects to their native city or their constituency.

The uproar of Partition along the new borders of the country dimly reverberated in Allahabad too, as tension prevailed between Hindus and Muslims in certain quarters of the town. A few of its citizens left for Pakistan. More than 10,000 refugees from Pakistan migrated to Allahabad. The suburb of Naini was sought to be developed by the Central Ministry of Relief and Rehabilitation as an industrial colony to accommodate these refugees. Gradually the trade in textiles, medicines, automobile parts, etc. came to be dominated by them. They were seamlessly integrated into the city's social fabric, although unlike some other Indian cities, the socio-cultural life of Allahabad never came to be dominated by the migrant community.

National Politics and Allahabad

The issues which broadly dominated national politics influenced the political life of Allahabad too. Nowhere was it made more dramatically manifest than in the clash between Nehru and that section of Congress leadership which was called the Rightists, led by Vallabhbhai Patel. Congress had a long history of tussle between these two groups and it deeply influenced the policies of the first Indian government at Delhi. It can be said that some of these policies were an act of faith for Nehru, particularly the issue of a secular polity. The assassination of Gandhi had temporarily brought a truce between Nehru and Patel and their long years of relationship ensured that a dignity was maintained by them even when they viscerally disagreed with one another. They shared a deep anguish at the passing away of the man who had been a spiritual father to them both. Allahabad saw the shaken men as they came, accompanied by the Congress leadership, for the immersion of Gandhi's ashes in the waters of the Sangam, the confluence of the Ganga and the Yamuna.

1 *opposite*
Smriti-vahan, the lorry which carried the ashes of Mahatma Gandhi for immersion in the Sangam. Now preserved in the Allahabad Museum, it is taken out every February 12, on an annual commemorative drive along a fixed route. Courtesy Allahabad Museum.

2 Govind Ballabh Pant and Sardar Patel seated on the lorry carrying Gandhi's ashes for immersion in the Sangam, 1948. Courtesy Allahabad Museum.

However, as the ashes of the Mahatma were gradually borne towards the sea, his cementing influence between Nehru and Patel seemed to weaken and a series of crises followed. The war in Kashmir and a mass migration of Hindus from East Bengal in 1950 had been raising communal tempers in northern India and Nehru became uncomfortable with many of his colleagues regarding their outlook on the Indian government's avowed policy of secularism. One such colleague was Purushottam Das Tandon, a prominent Congress leader from Allahabad. The fact that they both hailed from the same city did not obtrude on their political stand. Nehru wrote to Govind Ballabh Pant, the Chief Minister of Uttar Pradesh, in anguish: "U.P. is becoming a foreign land for me …. The U.P. Congress Committee functions in a manner which amazes me. Its voice is not the voice of the Congress I have known, but something which I have opposed for the greater part of my life. Purushottam Das Tandon, for whom I have the greatest affection and respect, is continually delivering speeches which seem to be opposed to the basic principles of the Congress."[1]

When Tandon was supported by Patel and his group in his bid for the Presidency of the All-India Congress Committee, Nehru gave public expression to his opinion that Tandon was unsuitable for the position. It seemed that not only Allahabad but the country itself was proving to be electorally not big enough to accommodate the divergence in the basic approaches of Nehru and Tandon as to the way the country should be run. Nehru wrote to Tandon: "Unfortunately you have become to large numbers of people in India some kind of symbol of this communal and revivalist outlook and the question rises in my mind: Is the Congress going that way also?"[2]

Notwithstanding Nehru's opposition, the election, viewed as a vicarious tussle between Nehru and Patel, ended in Tandon's victory. The intrigues continued after Patel's death and Tandon became more assertive. Nehru joined the battle more determinedly and subsequently resigned from the Working Committee and the Central Election Committee in a tactic to pressure Tandon to step down. The differences in their outlook were legion – going back to the time when Nehru had succeeded Tandon as the Chairman of the Allahabad Municipal Board in 1924. Almost 30 years later, as Prime Minister, Nehru asked his colleagues: "Which viewpoint and outlook are to prevail in the Congress – Tandon's or mine?" Tandon resigned and eventually retired to Allahabad, thus ending the first challenges posed to the Nehru-Gandhis from their home turf, Allahabad.

Till his death in 1964, Nehru remained the unchallenged leader in Allahabad and the rest of the country with an unstained reputation. His concern for integrity could also be seen in his dealings in Allahabad. In his very first year as Prime Minister, he was so agitated over complaints of corruption which had been levelled against a judge of the Allahabad High Court that he elected to personally remonstrate with the judge rather than create an unsavoury precedent of an inquiry being held. However he was not successful and the judge resigned only after he was removed from the Bench by the then Federal Court of India in 1949 after the inquiry that Nehru had tried to avert. When the Allahabad Municipality assessed his ancestral house at quite a low figure for the calculation of wealth tax in 1957, Nehru wrote to the Finance Minister and had it raised by almost five times.

His daughter Indira also remained very actively involved with Allahabad. During the 1957 elections, in addition to her responsibilities at the national level, she took particular interest in her father's constituency. Nehru wrote to his sister Vijayalakshmi about his daughter's election campaign in the city: "Hardly eating and often carrying on with a handful of peanuts and a banana, she has been constantly on the move, returning after midnight, flushed, slightly gaunt but full of spirit and with flashing eyes."[3]

Throughout the Nehru era Allahabad felt that Nehru belonged to it and Nehru himself never allowed the bonds to loosen. As long as Tandon lived Nehru maintained a cordial relationship with him and on more than one occasion called on the ailing leader at his home when he lay sick. They had high praise for each other in spite of their differences. Tandon's influence over the Allahabad electorate was immense and the Jan Sangh polled its lowest percentage of vote share in the KAVAL[4] towns in all

3
Purushottam Das Tandon (1882–1962). Courtesy Allahabad Museum.

4
Jawaharlal Nehru and Lal Bahadur Shastri walking alongside the lorry carrying Gandhi's ashes, 1948. Courtesy Allahabad Museum.

5
Lal Bahadur Shastri's favourite chair in the verandah of his Allahabad house on Katghar Road.

the legislative assembly elections till 1967, mainly due to his influence.

However it was not as if other political parties did not have a presence in Allahabad. The CPI had considerable influence over the Allahabad University Students' Union. The old CPI office in Johnstongunj, under which a couple of cycle shops have opened, is even today called Subhash Hall in memory of one of its Allahabad unit members, Subhash Mukhopadhyaya, who was killed in police firing in Ballia in 1950 while participating in a protest rally organized by the Party opposing the legitimacy of the Indian state in what came to be termed as the Ranadive line in party formulations. An old Party member, G.P. Singh, recalls how he was initiated into Marxism while a student of the Ewing Christian College in Allahabad. With the Party being banned, copies of the Party organ *Crossroads* used to be pasted on the walls of a building across the road at night and the young students would feel a thrill of adventure as they came out of their hostels to read the pages early the next morning. Eric Higgins, a handsome young teacher of the school, made Goldsmith come alive in the classroom while in the evenings a handful of students would gather in the coffee house of the school to hear him quietly expound Marxism to them. Later, while a student of Holland Hall of the University, Singh would meet with other students after dinner in a house called Gulab Bhavan to listen to night-long lectures on social philosophy by the brilliant Marxist P.C. Joshi, who had been removed as CPI General Secretary and had moved to Allahabad during 1951–52 after having fallen out with the Party leadership. Joshi returned to Delhi soon afterwards, rehabilitated in the Party.

Lohia also wielded a strong influence in the University and the Students' Union came to be largely dominated by the Lohia-ists after the anti-English-language movement of the '60s.

In the first few decades after Independence it was usual to find many bureaucrats from Allahabad in high positions in the Central government. They too perhaps represented the ethos of the city in a way, and it would be interesting to speculate what effect Allahabad had on national governance through them.

But the immediate effect exercised by Allahabad largely diminished with the deaths in close succession of Nehru and Shastri. As Prime Minister, Shastri had visited Allahabad five times in the course of about two years, being accorded a hero's welcome after the war of 1965. When Shastri's ashes returned to Allahabad, virtually the entire city came out on the streets to pay homage to another of its distinguished sons.

Nehru's death had left the political scene open to uncertainty, leading to speculation and conjecture when Indira Gandhi stepped into the role. The results of the 1967 elections provided further fuel to controversial postures and the comparatively weak showing of the Congress dramatically increased the number of prime-ministerial hopefuls who chose to openly deride the Prime Minister as the "dumb doll" of the Indian Parliament. Analysts like Rajni Kothari saw the beginning of "a period of collective leadership and team work".[5] But here perhaps the mood of the Indian Parliament was not in sync with that of the Indian electorate. Indira, by choosing to remain aloof from the intra-party squabbles which beset the Congress, emerged as a sort of conciliator and national figure and added an international dimension to her political persona by her foreign tours. She continued to visit Allahabad as well. Her clash with the Congress Party bosses over the Presidential elections of 1969 resulted in her victory and she proceeded to further consolidate her position by taking radical steps like the nationalization of banks and the abolition of the privy purses of the former Indian princes. Her landslide election victory in 1971 provided her with an unrivalled position. As a prominent historian has commented: "In this sense politics since Nehru's death may be described as India looking for a leader like Tibetans searching for a reincarnation, and, in 1971, their discovery of one."[6]

"Allahabad's daughter", as the city liked to think of her, was lionized and feted lavishly when she arrived for a visit to the city after the victorious war of 1971 with Pakistan. As a child I have a clear memory

6
A statue of Indira Gandhi stands just ahead of a market named after Hemvati Nandan Bahuguna close to Bahuguna's bungalow in Ashok Nagar.

Nehru and Later

161

7
Hemvati Nandan Bahuguna's charismatic politics had marked him out as a possible Prime Ministerial candidate, but this was not to be. The fencing round a park encircling his statue is adorned here with Congress flags.

of her driving down from the airport in an open black limousine through roads which had been decorated with flowers, lights, and buntings. She stood with folded hands and her security guard, behind her, personally stretched out his hands and took the garlands which enthusiastic supporters tried to put around her neck. His briskness made quite an impression on my mind and I heard elders remarking on the tight security surrounding the Prime Minister, which now sounds ironical in the face of her assassination at the hands of her own bodyguards amidst botched-up security arrangements. I grew bold and asked for some of the paper flowers which were being taken down by volunteers and was properly rebuked by my aunts and uncles. However, later in the evening, we found that the flowers had been quietly placed inside our gate in generous measure by the volunteers before they left. As it was known that Mrs Gandhi would be returning to Delhi on the same night, we reverently kept watch to catch a glimpse of her cavalcade on the now almost deserted road. This time she was driven in a blue sedan at high speed. It can be said that her visit inaugurated a new culture of political sycophancy in the city. It demonstrated the limits to which city politicians were willing to go in incurring huge expenses for welcoming leaders on state visits. After a year or so Hemvati Nandan Bahuguna was accorded a similarly opulent welcome when he visited his home city as Chief Minister. But these lavish affairs could not gloss over the reflection of political discontent which simmered in Allahabad, much as it did in many parts of the country.

The 1971 war brought blackouts to Allahabad and I remember listening to the clip-clop of army pack-horses throughout the night and day. India's victory over her western neighbour was symbolized by the army convoys carrying prisoners of war to their detention camps, some of which were located in the city. The vanquished soldiers sat cross-legged, with heads bowed, as Gurkha soldiers stood guard over them. It was rumoured that a few of these detenues subsequently managed to escape and were said to have been recaptured in the Muslim quarters of the city. The ready acceptance of the rumours reminded one that the war across national boundaries could without great difficulty be vicariously transferred between two ethnic communities inhabiting the cities of a nation which prided itself on a composite heritage and culture.

Indira was at the pinnacle of her power in the aftermath of the '71 war, "a goddess Durga in conflict",[7] "a Kautilya in counsel". Both the head of the Central government as well as the head of the Uttar Pradesh government were extremely charismatic and capable, and both hailed from Allahabad. But very soon a silent antagonism grew between them. Mrs Gandhi suspected Bahuguna of harbouring prime-ministerial ambitions and Bahuguna's adroit moves at consolidating his position added grist to the mill of political rumour.

Meanwhile Jai Prakash Narayan emerged as a rallying point for the divided opposition and new forms of grassroots protest seemed to be emerging in the country. Allahabad may find mention as a prominent place for such forms of dissent and reform. The restive atmosphere in the city somewhat caught JP's imagination and in spite of governmental obstructions the All India Youth Conference was held in a local college in June 1974. A "sense of imminent revolution" and profound unrest was building up and found expression in intense political discourses among intellectuals, writers, and political activists creating a mood of great engagement and dialogue. Demonstrations and rising criticism of the government were the order of the day. "The flashpoint came with an Allahabad court's decision on an electoral petition against Mrs Gandhi from the last election."[8]

It was a different image of "Nehru's daughter" that began to dominate the political camps in the city. It therefore seemed poetic justice to many that it was the Allahabad High Court that delivered the first constitutional rebuke to the arrogance of the coterie who surrounded Mrs Gandhi and who fully expected a sympathetic verdict. But in that room numbered 27 at the Allahabad High Court, in the dramatic words of Rahi Masoom Raza's novel on the Emergency, *Katra Bi Arzoo*: "the dream of the founding fathers of the Indian republic allegorically waited with bated breath …. Many people had forgotten the important fact that they stood in Allahabad High Court and Allahabad High Court is famous for verdicts against the government, whether of the English or of the Congress."[9]

On June 12, 1975 the Court set aside Indira Gandhi's election to the Lok Sabha in 1971, leaving the entire country stunned. The immediate appeal of the Prime Minister to the Supreme Court resulted in a vacation bench, through an interim ruling, permitting her to remain in office but not to vote or participate in the proceedings of Parliament.

There can be perhaps no two opinions on what that other Allahabadian, Nehru, would have done in similar circumstances. Nehru's daughter, however, provoked by the verdict and afraid of detractors, and with all her inborn obduracy hyperactive in the crisis, listened ultimately to her coterie and not to the saner counsels echoing her father's ideals. And barely 13 days from the High Court judgement, accompanied by a single minister, S.S. Ray, she went to the President at midnight to ask for a declaration of a state of Emergency. The President "asked no questions and signed the proclamation".[10] The Cabinet was presented with a fait accompli at a meeting held early the next morning, and knowing that all the leading lights of the Opposition were already in prison, buckled and acquiesced in her decision.

8
Indira's room in Anand Bhavan.

In an earlier, more optimistic age Allahabad had rejoiced as one of its sons appealed to the nation "at the stroke of the midnight hour" to "join with faith and confidence in this great adventure … to build the noble mansion of free India."[11] Three eventful decades later, it was in some sense a bitter tragedy for the city that one of its illustrious daughters should have chosen to undo so much of her father's legacy at the same midnight hour.

NOTES

1   S. Gopal, *Jawaharlal Nehru: A Biography*, Vol. 2, Delhi, 1983, p. 92.

2   Ibid., p. 93.

3   Ibid., Vol. 3, p. 67.

4   Kanpur, Agra, Varanasi, Allahabad, Lucknow: the five prominent cities of UP.

5   Rajni Kothari, *Politics, Mainly Indian*, Delhi, 1978, p. 315.

6   Percival Spear, *A History of India*, Vol. 2, Harmondsworth, 1984, p. 261.

7   According to her formidable opponent, Atal Behari Vajpayee.

8   Spear, p. 266.

9   Rahi Masoom Raza, *Katra Bi Arzoo*, Delhi, (1978) 2000, p. 123, translated from the Hindi.

10   I. Malhotra, *Indira Gandhi: A Personal and Political Memoir*, London, 1989, p. 169.

11   Nehru's address to the nation on the eve of Independence, August 14, 1947.

9
Nehru's room in Anand Bhavan.

Neelum Saran Gour

A New Triveni

Neelum Saran Gour

Allahabad's relationship with the Raj remained a complicated one in which reverse colonial nostalgia competed with retrospective triumph. Despite its frontline participation in the National Movement, Allahabad remained a strikingly anglicized place in which the norms and forms of colonial life were kept alive by a dominant social class. Street names in the Civil Lines changed but their former names continued to be used rather more than their new ones – Clive, Auckland, Elgin, Strachey, Stanley, Thornhill, Colvin, Hastings, Drummond. Only old Allahabad hands now know who the men were (mostly governors, lieutenant-governors, civil servants, or judges) after whom the streets were named. It didn't matter. The names had become part of the city's personality, detached from their physical owners. For Allahabad was attached to its Raj romance, the subtly choreographed ceremony of empire with its round of garden parties, dances, plays, tennis tournaments, flower and dog shows, gymkhana club meets, and church socials. And its Raj anecdotage about Brit civil servants who cared, judges who were sticklers for rightness, and those great British teachers – witty, painstaking, and inspiring.

My own favourites include Augustus S. Harrison, the first Principal of Muir Central College, who rode around the city on a tricycle, and Samuel Alexander Hill, who taught chemistry at Muir and lived in a gracious old villa called Belvedere House opposite the Senate House campus. The picture that offers itself to instant revival, when looking back on the Raj, is that of Rudyard Kipling walking across to Belvedere from his own bungalow close by to play what he liked to call "Allahabadminton".[1] Or Kipling sitting in the deep stone-paved verandah of Hill's house, writing "The Man Who Would Be King" (1888).[2] When Hill died in 1891, crowds of grieving students sought permission to carry the coffin to the hearse-van and accompany it to the "gora kabristan".[3] This image stays with me as a powerful metaphor of Allahabad's ambivalent relationship with the Raj. But as the looking-back generation aged and retired, a language movement foregrounding Hindi had raised its voice and the Civil Service had permitted aspiring candidates to write their examinations in their regional languages if they preferred. Post-Emergency, a cultural shift began. Mandir, Mandal, and McDonalds became the new Triveni that overflowed and submerged the former city.

A city where secularism was ensouled before the word was known, Allahabad had its communal skirmishes but these were relatively few and far between. There were always powerful forces actively countering the subterranean build-up of religion-related differences.

1 *opposite*
The city that was. A quiet stretch of Elgin Road a quarter-century ago, now extensively built over and noisy with traffic. Courtesy John Harrison.

2
Colonial bungalows being demolished.

3
Rickshaws carrying hoardings advertising coaching institutes, Allahabad's new "industry".

168

Neelum Saran Gour

For example, just before the 1888 Congress Session in Allahabad a meeting was held on June 20 at which Munshi Fazal Ali Khan of Daryabad appealed to the Allahabad Muslims not to be misled by the pro-British Syed Ahmad Khan's influence and asked them to attend the forthcoming Congress Session in great numbers. Soon afterwards, in September of the same year, Swami Alaram addressed Allahabad Hindus and asked them to cooperate with the Congress.[4]

But it wasn't easy going. In his memoirs Sayyad Muzaffar Hasan who was closely connected with the Kadariya Sufi sect at the Daira Shah Rafiullah and was an active "Congress Muslim" (as against a "League Muslim") records how hard it was for him to enter hard-core Muslim areas without being abused or stoned, and how difficult it was for "secular Muslims" like him to even bury their dead in Muslim graveyards. The hard-core Hindu was scarcely any better. He mentions how his friend, Sayyad Nazeer Ali Zaidi was spat on, sprayed with red betel juice, by an opinionated Hindu. Before the Partition, he recounts with great

[4] The city home of Vishwanath Pratap Singh, another Prime Minister of Allahabad origin.

A New Triveni

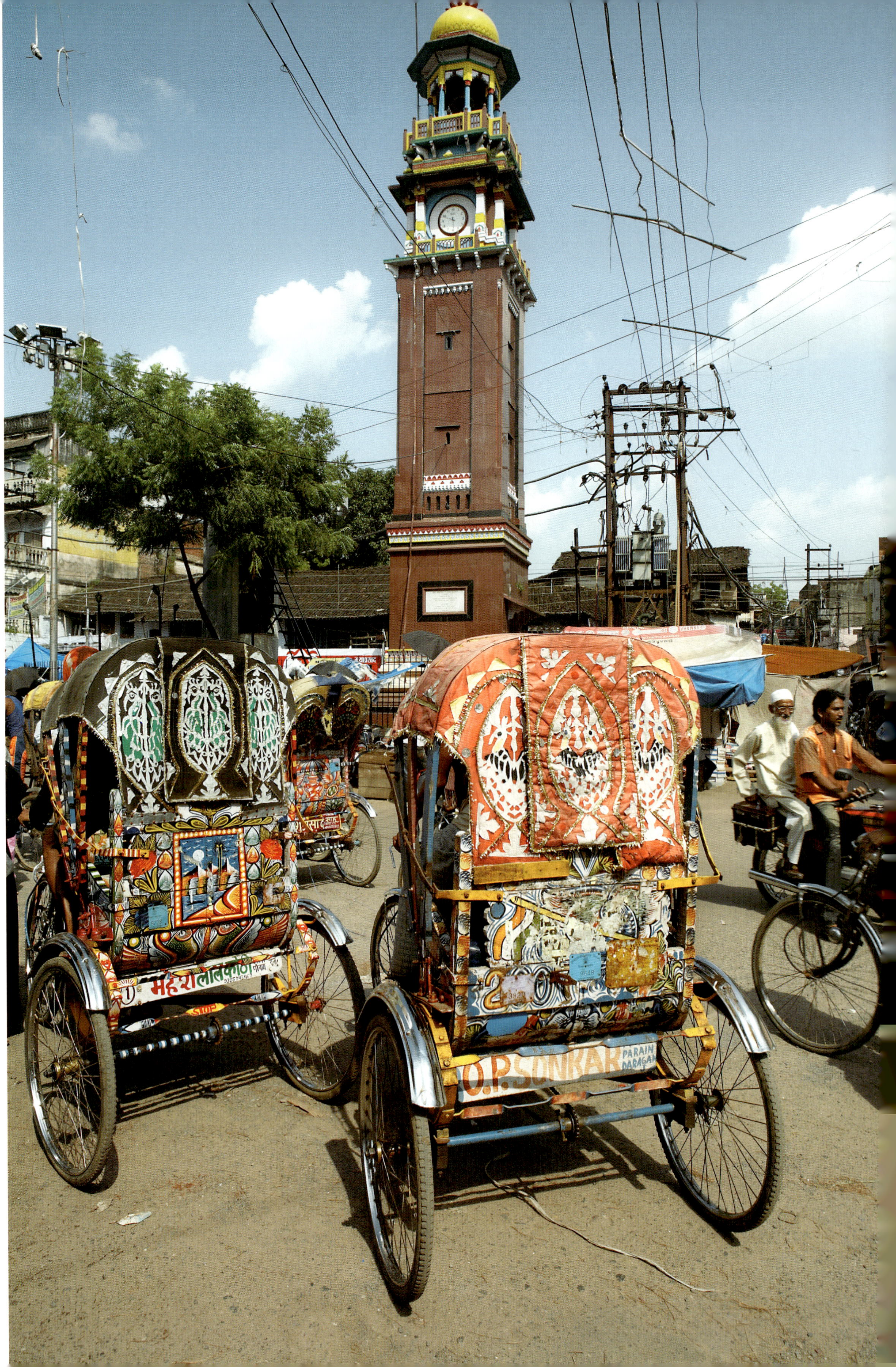

candour, Muslim mobs roamed the lanes, shouting "*Has ke lenge Pakistan, larh ke lenge Hindustan!*" and "*Dhoti-raj nahin chalega, choti-raj nahin chalega!*" (We'll laugh and take Pakistan [effortlessly], we'll fight and take Hindustan, and Down with the rule of the dhoti- and *choti*-wearers [Hindus]).[5]

Himself an outcast, jailed many times and subjected to all the toughest rigours of prison in British India, Hasan's career stands out as a potent confirmation of the existence of a committed species of nationalist Muslim, of which Allahabad always had a strong contingent. Not for nothing was this city dear to Dara Shikoh, who translated the *Upanishads* into Persian, and not for nothing was Allahabad the city of 12 Sufi centres since medieval times.

There can be no better example of this synthesis than in the person of Mirza Abul Fazal, Nehru's close associate in the Allahabad Municipality, who held an MA degree in both Sanskrit and Arabic from Dhaka University and a PhD on the parities between the *Rig Veda* and the *Quran* from Berlin University. Mirza had named his children Sita Fatima and Krishna Muhammad. But as social dispensations are no respecters of idealism, Mirza was persecuted by Muslim right-wingers for his English translation of the *Quran* for the Nizam of Hyderabad's Religious Endowment Trust, and was reduced to great penury and forced to make a living by selling buffalo milk. (Where in Allahabad can one go without the ubiquitous cow or

6
A busy market behind the Chowk clock-tower.

5 *opposite*
The clock-tower at Chowk Gangadas, built by the Rani Mandi merchant-bankers and designed by Sir Swinton Jacob.

A New Triveni

7
Lawyers heading for the High Court. In the park behind is a statue of an empowered Eklavya drawing his bow against the entrenched establishment. An eloquent representation of political power-shifts in the city.

buffalo sharing historical space with the greats?)⁶

The point I am trying to make is that "secular Allahabad" was a real thing, ante-dating Nehru, though Nehru's personal credibility as a leader stamped the philosophy with his name. Alongside was the strong right-wing on both sides, impervious to softer philosophies of coexistence.

Nowhere is Nehru's credibility better demonstrated than in an incident in Chowk in 1936, some days before Muharram. A pig's head had been found in an Atarsuiya mosque and a large crowd of enraged Muslims gathered near Nakhas Kohna and Rani Mandi. An equal number of Hindus waited at Atarsuiya and Loknath. The British Collector arrived, inspected the scene, had the pig's head removed and gave reassurances of proper action against the offenders. As soon as he left, all hell broke loose and bricks began falling with deadly aim. Suddenly a tonga was sighted, coming from the Kotwali side. Pandit Nehru alighted with some companions. He held a stick in his hand. The mobs froze. On the Rani Mandi side waited the vengeful Muslim mob, on the Loknath side the fierce Hindus. Nehru went striding down the Rani Mandi lane, waving the stick at the mobs, fiercely glaring at the crowds. He walked all the way to Daira-e Shah Ajmal and met Yusuf Bhai and Shahid Fakhri, the *sajjadanasheen* ("the one who occupies the prayer mat") of the Daira and an active Congressman himself. Then he strode back the way he had come and climbed onto the waiting tonga. Before the tonga clip-clopped away, Nehru glared at both mobs one last time, raised his voice and shouted "*Bharat Mata ki Jai!*" The tonga faded from view. The mobs dispersed quietly. Muharram, three days later, was peaceful and a banner near the Kotwali proclaimed "We, the Hindus of Allahabad, are with our Muslim brothers on this day of mourning."⁷

It may sound like a cloying saccharine sequence from a Bollywood film to a present-day cynic, but it actually happened. There *were* forces that overruled sectarian animosity and there did exist people unaffected by it. Akbar Ilahabadi, the city's

8
Two chapters in the city's history – a contemporary steel-and-glass high-rise alongside a colonial block.

9
Bicycles lined up outside a popular coaching institute.

A New Triveni

173

legendary Urdu voice, could shrug off the matter thus:

Mazhabi bahas maine ki hi nahin
Faltu aql mujhmein thi hi nahin.
(I never did go in for religious wranglings
Having no extra wits to waste.)

So much so that on August 14, 1947, Syed Mahbub Ali's diary entry states blandly that it was the 26th day of Ramzan, that India was now free, that the new country had been named Pakistan, and that he had hosted a party for fellow lawyers at the Bar Association, at which the famous Allahabad chef, Sakir, outdid himself. More telling is his entry a week later, on August 21, in which he relates how he took some dainties to his jailed friend, Khush-hal Chandra Nigam, who was a diehard member of the Hindu Mahasabha, obdurately against the Congress and Muslims in particular. He writes that he had to wait at the Naini Jail till two in the afternoon and that his friend was delighted with the dainties. This little inset in the larger canvas illustrates another side to Allahabad's communal scene – how close personal relationships continued to flourish alongside ideological oppositions. It is a persisting paradox and a vastly reassuring one.

I read that Allahabad Muslims resettled in Karachi have formed an NGO called the Allahabad Social Welfare Association, that Karachi Allahabadis long to revisit the Kumbh Mela and that many senior members come annually to the old city with gifts of lawn cloth and dry fruits and return with Loknath namkins and Allahabad guavas. One of them, Sheikh Shahid Hussain, wistfully resorts to quoting a couplet:

Hamarey shahar ko maqtal bana diya kisne?
Suna hai ahle-siyasat ki meherbani hai.
(Who has made a slaughter-house of our city?
I have heard it is by the grace of politics.)[8]

After Babri, parallel currents of coexistence and unrest subsist. The global climate of terror strikes and ethnic mistrust has left the city in a state of cautious stasis and growing polarization of communities in which, beneath all the surface discoursing, there is an uneasy silence and a mood of loss and doubt whether events have outpaced and defeated us, our secularism discredited by both its opponents and its champions.

In a region which hosted and absorbed so many incoming "others", from Greeks, Sakas, Parthians, and Huns to Turks, Afghans, Mughals, and Europeans, whose presence constantly challenged settled sanctities, a generic sense of identity and difference was inevitable. Always a clannish sort of place in caste matters, Allahabad had its entrenched power and pressure lobbies and associated subcultures organized along caste lines. There was the Kayastha Pathshala bastion, the Malaviya-Kashmiri Pandit brahmin lobby, a tough and focused Vaishya group, and maybe a somewhat smaller Thakur fraternity with its roots in nearby Jaunpur. But when Vishwanath Pratap Singh, yet another Prime Minister of Allahabad origin, implemented the proposals of the Mandal Commission, he brought to a boil forces that had been simmering a long time. The leaders whose counter-ideologies formed the bedrock of anti-Congress protest from Ram Manohar Lohia to Jai Prakash Narayan had all advanced a programme for the assimilation of the so-called "dalits", and the centring of the hitherto marginalized led to power shifts and relocations in the city, as in the rest of UP and indeed the entire country. It changed the demography of Allahabad as rural migrants, especially a floating dalit student population, began pouring in from the nearby villages, even as the younger generation of "caste-Hindu" families began migrating to the metro-cities, lured by prospects of lucrative jobs in private companies where the rules of quota-reservation did not operate.

With the dismantling of colonial structures, Allahabad was no longer a slightly elitist city but rather an arena for the newly empowered classes, mindful of freshly granted privileges and impunities. The mushrooming coaching institutes are concrete markers of the rise of a new aspirational student community in a time of bitterly savage competition for limited options. This subaltern city, confused by its present and clueless about its future, has become necessarily past-obsessed.

In the history of human rights this incoherence may only be a symptom of an ultimately meaningful transition as the city mirrors expressions of confidence in hitherto invisible segments of humanity, even as it seems chaotic, tawdry, and gone to seed. Allahabad has seen many demographic shifts, influxes, and displacements. In the fullness of time the present may well be the expected fruition of forces in a mutating democracy. The boy who comes from a village and who knows neither formal Hindi and certainly no English but only the dialect of some rural pocket, picks up computer skills rapidly and may even be the representative of a new category of evolving social material that history will record on its credit side. In moments of chivalry this does seem to be so and the losses brought on by a seeming civilizational lull worth the losing, were it not for the current migration of impunity from the ruling classes to a hyperactive underworld sharing power with elected leaders, making Allahabad slowly sink into the badlands of UP.

The *subah* was always a defiant and lawless one, as Mughal sources constantly testify. During Aurangzeb's time "the deteriorating law and order situation was a constant source of worry...." Even soldiers who had gone without a salary turned violent, "entered the fort of Allahabad and by force seized the imperial treasury".[9]

So unruly was the area that Saif Khan, the *subahdar*, was so "disappointed with the existing condition ... that in sheer helplessness he requested the emperor for his transfer from the Subah".[10] Writing about the defiant zamindars, Manucci recorded, "we were some days in Allahabad, and the Governor was Bahadur Khan, who was absent on a campaign against some villagers who objected to pay their revenue without, at least, one fight".[11]

On less optimistic days it does seem that old anarchic forces have been let loose, and the dark laws hibernating in history's basement, which bide their time during spells when military and administrative dispensations make temporary order prevail, but once the hold slackens, leap into action. Then Allahabad does feel like a former outpost of civilization reclaimed by the encircling jungle, closing in to stifle all the monuments of its former graciousness and quiet civility that was no surface veneer but the refined blend of three old cultures.

When globalization burst upon the scene, old Allahabad was already witnessing its dismemberment – colonial bungalows and havelis being razed to the ground and nondescript apartment blocks mushrooming; tranquil, tree-lined streets invaded by garish markets; large gardens plotted into petrol stations, cyber-cafes, fast-food eateries, coaching institutes, indifferent nursing homes. The language went too – Allahabad's former pure Sanskritized Hindi that seamlessly blended into elegant Urdu and, in certain circles, perfect, polished, if somewhat bookish English, not to forget its lively, spicy leaven of regional slang, flamboyantly incestuous, scatological, perverse, provocative, and funny.

When the very first shopping mall opened, seemingly the whole city turned up to ride on the escalators! This postmodern globalized present with its multiplexes, its McDonalds, and its mobile phone chatter may not really be a levelling down of cultural individuality into one faceless anonymity. In the past, cities have engaged in and retrieved their identities through many tides of "globalization" – though it may have functioned under different names. It remains to be seen what will survive this one when the honeymoon is over and our cities disengage themselves from the heady embrace and reassert an approximate ante-global personality. A great deal may be lost or filtered out but what survives may be said to have passed the essential identity test. For Allahabad the sangam of global and local shall take some time to reveal the chemistry of its waters.

10
Allahabad's rivers continue to be its symbols of constancy in the flux of history.

We were always told in school that the longitude 82½° East passed through Allahabad and that the rest of India got its Indian Standard Time from our city. Only recently I learnt that this longitude doesn't actually cross Allahabad but is elsewhere, east of the city! Just as the old Allahabadis aren't here but elsewhere, everywhere, products of a diaspora that is laden with memories and sentimental connections. I used to liken Allahabad to a metaphoric oxbow lake, a crescent-shaped pool of standing water left behind by the mainstream when the large, meandering river of development abandoned one of its big loops and changed its course. The pool may silt up, as so many did in Mesolithic times. Or something new and living may emerge from the renewed soil.

One of Allahabad's greatest musical legends, Janki Bai, was a national celebrity, whose singing was acclaimed by connoisseurs and lay audiences about the first 30 years of the 20th century but is relatively neglected now, until recently preserved only in rare lac records playable on old trumpet turntables. Janki Bai always ended her performance with the words: "*Main hoon Janki Bai Ilahabadi* ('I am Miss Janki Bai of Ilahabad')." That ring of certitude in belonging is something that any diasporic or resident Allahabadi might want to cheer.

I certainly would.

NOTES

1 Arvind Krishna Mehrotra, *The Last Bungalow – Writings on Allahabad*, Penguin India, New Delhi, 2007, p. 101.

2 Ibid., p. 107.

3 B.S. Gehlot, *Ilahabad – Ve Din Ve Log*, Raka Prakashan, Allahabad, 2000, p. 67.

4 Ibid., p. 174.

5 Ibid., p. 46.

6 Ibid., p. 303.

7 Ibid., p. 16.

8 *Hindustan Times, Allahabad Live*, May 3, 2006.

9 Surendra Nath Sinha, *Subah of Allahabad Under the Great Mughals,* Jamia Millia Islamia, New Delhi, 1974, p. 75.

10 Ibid.

11 Ibid., p. 112.

Index

Figures in bold denote captions

Abdul Alim Asi Sikandarpuri 151
Abdul Wadud, Qazi 147
'Abdullah Katib, Mir 49, 52, 58, 67
Abdullah, Mir 58, 67
Abhyudaya 99
Abul Fazl 22, 45, 46, 48
Abu'l Hasan 58, 62, **62**, 68
Abul Hasan Amrullah Ilahabadi 147, 150, 151
Adeeb 155
Agarwal, Bharat Bhushan 142
Ahmad Ali 154
Ahmad Khan, Syed **92**, 119, 153, 169
Ajneya, S.H. Vatsyayan 108, 142
Ajodhya Nath, Pandit 96, 99
Akbar Ilahabadi **151**, 152, 153, 172
Akshaya-vata **13**, 14, 15, 24, **127**, 137
Alaram, Swami 169
Alfred Park **77**, 79, **80**, 84, **89**, **91**, 98, 139
Ali Hussain 27
All India Khilafat Conference 98
All Saints' Cathedral **75**, 78
Allahabad Bank 27, **73**, 79
Allahabad Club 79, 82, 85
Allahabad Flour Mill 79
Allahabad Fort **20**, 46, **46**, 48, **48**, 49, **49**, 73, 75, 87, 90
Ashoka's Pillar 20, **20**
Allahabad High Court 28, 78, 81, 82, 85, 92, 114–25, **115–17**, **119–21**, **123**, 159, 164, **172**
Allahabad Museum **26**, **44**, 77, **87**, **92**, **94**, **99**, **124**, **140–42**, **152**, **153**, **157–59**
Allahabad Secretariat 78
Allahabad University **6**, **23–25**, 81, 84, 85, 96, 100, **103**, **104**, 105, 107, 115, 127–30, **127**, 133, **133**, **134**, **134**, 136, 137, 139–41, 143–45, 153, 160, 167
Allen, George **74**, 82
Alopi Bagh 84, 87, 88
Alopi Devi Temple **17**
Alston, Charles Ross 120
Amarkant 113
Amir Hasan Dihlawi 58, **60**, 66, 68
Amiruddin Ahmad 147
Anand Bhavan 94, **94**, **96–98**, **100**, **101**, 103, 153, **164**, **165**
Anandi Lal 27
Anglo-Indians 75, 77, **79**, 82
Aqa Reza **57**, 58, 59, **59**, **61**, 62, 68
Arathoon, H.W. 120
Ardh Kumbh 35, 38, 40, 41
Arifi 57, 67, **67**, 68

Arratoon, M.J. 82
Asghar Gondvi 155
Ashk, Upendranath 154
Ashok Nagar **161**
Asthana, Narayan Prasad 121, 155
Atarsuiya 145, 172
Azad Hind Fauj 96

Baburam 28
Bachchan, Harivansh Rai 103, 113, 133, 142, **143**, 145
Bade Hanumanji Temple **16**
Baghambaris 37
Bahuguna, H.N. 101, 161, **162**, 163
Banaras Hindu University **94**, 122
Banerji, A.C. 133
Banerji, Durga Charan 122
Banerji, P.C. 82, 110, 120
Banerji, S.C. 121
Bank Road 103
Baptists 74
Begum Bagh/Bahadurgunj 54
Bengal/i 73, 89, 110, 119–21, 141, 158
Beni Prasad 133
Bennet, Edward 117
Besant, Annie 98, 100
Bhagat Singh 96
Bhagavata cult 20
Bharadwaja Ashram 25, 26, **29**
Bharat 99
Bharati, Dharamvir 113, 133, 144
Bharti Bhavan Library **144**
Bhatnagar, Bahadur Singh 54
Bhattacharya, Adityaram 134
Bhattagram **21**, 22
Bhita 12, **19**, 22
Bible House 81
Birbar, Raja 49, **50**
Bishambhar Nath, Pandit 96
Bishandas 63, 65, **65**, 66, 68
Bismil, Ram Prasad 96
Biswas, Satish Chandra 98
Bonnerjee, W.C. 96
Bose, Jyotin 98
Bose, Subhas Chandra 96, 98
Bower, John Knot 92
Buddha/Buddhism 18–20
Buddhaghosa 18
Buncombe's/Barnett's Hotel 82
Burhan 65

Calcutta University 120, 129, 140
Canning, Lord 75, **80**, 94
Canning Road 78, 82, 84, 108
Cantonment **6**, 88, 89
Cawnpore Road 79
Chamier, Edward 117
Chand 99
Chandra Shekhar 101
Chandra Shekhar Azad **91**, **92**, 98
Chapman, Captain 90–92
Chatham Lines 88
Chatterjee, Nityanand **79**, 98
Chattopadhyaya, Khetresh 133
Chaturvedi, Ram Swarup 113
Chaube, Shukradev 28

Chester, Charles 88
Chiene, O.M. 121
Chintamani, C.Y. 99
Chitralekha 107
Chowk 27, **73**, 74, **76**, 84, 100, **171**, 172
Chowk Gangadas 26, **144**, **171**
Christian Tract and Book Society 81
Civil Lines 78, **78**, 79, 82, 84, 85, 107, 110, 113, 122, 124, 167
Clive Road 108
Clive, Robert **46**, 167
Coffee House 107, 108, 110–13, **113**
Colonelgunj 73, 88, 103
Congress Party **92**, 94, 96, 98, 103, 119, 157, 158, 161, **162**, 169, 174
Cosmopolitan Club **79**, 98
Cox, Homersham 130, 133
Crawley, Thomas 79
Crosthwaite, Lt-Gov 119
Crosthwaite School 141
Curzon, Lord 52, 54, 117

Daira-e Shah Ajmal **150**, 151, **154**, 172
Daira-e Shah Rafiullah 169
Daira-e Sheikh Muhammadi Shah **6**
Daira-e Sheikh Muhibbullah Shah **149**
Daniell, Thomas **48**
Daraganj 88
Darbari Building 110
Dave Brothers 122
Dave, Sunder Lal 82, 98, **103**, 119, 122, 155
David, Ernest 120
Deb, R.N. 134
Deb, S.C. 113, 133
Deshbandhu 99
Dhar, Nil Ratan 103, 133
Dwarkanath "Gotewale" 27

East India Company 48, 73, 74, **80**, 94, 115, 116, 129, 139
Ehtesham Husain, Syed 155
Elgin Road **167**
Emerson, William **75**, 129, 130
Ewing Christian College 79, 81, 160

Fazal Ali Khan 169
Firaq, Raghupati Sahai 103, 104, 133, **153**, 154, 155
Freedom Movement 11, 87–101, 157, 167
Frizzoni & Co. **75**, 78, 79, 123

Gadhwa 12, **21**, 22
Gandhi, Feroze **100**
Gandhi, Indira 100, **100**, 101, 124, 159, 161, **161**, 163, 164
Gandhi, M.K. (Mahatma) 39, 78, **94**, **96**, **97**, 98, 100, 103, 104, 108, 110, 122, 140, 141, 153, 157, 158, **157–59**, 161
Gandhi, Rajiv **100**, 101
Ganga, river 11, 14, 15, **15–17**, 18, 22, 25, 26, 28, 31, **35**, 39, 41, 43, 48, 49, 73, 88, 90, 141, 147, 157

Ganganatha Jha Research Institute for Sanskrit Studies **77**
George Town 84
Ghulam Azam Afzal, Shah 150, 151
Ghulam Ghaus Bekhabar 152
Ghulam Qutbuddin Musib, Shah 150
Ghulam Yahya Insaf, Shah 151
Girai Chamar 100
Glynn-Griffiths, Dr 82
Gokhale, Gopal Krishna 94
Gorakh Prasad 133
Government Press 78, 81, 82
Grand Trunk Road 74
Gulab Bhavan 160
Gupt, Bhairav Prasad 113
Gupt, Shiv Prasad 99
Guptas 12, 15, **21**, 22, 49, 50
Gyanendra Kumar 155
Gyanranjan 145
Gymkhana Club **77**

Haldar, Asit Kumar **44**, **133**, 137
Handia 26
Hari Ram and Sons 110
Harrison, Augustus S. 167
Harshavardhana 22, **26**, 38
Haseer Azimabadi 155
Hastings Road 82, 123, 142
Higgins, Eric 160
Hill, Samuel Alexander 167
Hindi Sahitya Sammelan 139, **139**
Hindustan Review 81, 99
Hindustani 155
Hindustani Academy **77**, **140**, 153, 155
Holy Trinity Church 74, **74**, 85
Husain, Syed Aijaz 154
Husain, Ustad 68, **68**

Ikoba, Yogmata Kiko 41
(The) Independent 99
Indian Herald 99
Indian Press 139
Iswar Saran 121

Jacob, Swinton 27, 128, **171**
Jagati's 107
Jai Ma Mandavi Devi Ramlila Mandal 27
Jain, Gian Chand 155
Jain, Nemichandra 142
Jami Masjid 54
Janki Bai 177
Jennings, J.G. **133**, 137
Jesuits 51, 58
Jha, Amaranatha 103, 133, **136**, 155
Jha, Ganganatha 133
Jhunsi 12, 18, **18**, 22, 25
Johnstongunj 160
Joona Akhara 41
Joshi, Murli Manohar 101
Joshi, P.C. 160
Joshi, Shekhar 113

Kalidas 14
Kalyan Singh 125

Kanji Sahai Mateen 152
Kara-Manikpur 22, 45, 46, 48
Karmayogi 99
Katghar Road **160**
Katju, Kailash Nath 99
Katra 73, 82, 84
Kaushambi 18–20, **20**, **21**, 22, 133
Kayastha Pathshala 120, 174
Kesavdas 62, 63, 65, 66
Khairuddin Ilahabadi 147
Khuldabad Sarai 54
Khusrau Bagh 52, 54, 89
Kipling, Rudyard 74, **74**, 81, 167
Kothari, Rajni 161
Kotwali 76, **87**, **105**, 172
Kripalani, Acharya **97**, 99, 103
Krishnan, K.S. 133
Kumbh Mela **6**, 25, **30**, **31**, 31, 35, 43, 174
Kunzru, Hriday Nath 155
Kydgunj 52, 73, **90**

Lajpat Rai, Lala 94
Lakshminarain, Lala 27
Laurie's Hotel 78, 79
[The] Leader 81, 99
Liaqat Ali, Maulvi 89
Lohia, Ram Manohar 99, 108, 160, 174
Loknath **110**, **111**, 172, 174
Lowther Castle 96
Lukergunj 139
Lyall, Sir Alfred 129

Madho Prasad 121
Magh/Mela 22, 25, **26**, 31, **33**, 39, 77
Mahamandaleshwars 36, **40**, 41
Mahanirvanis 37
Mahavira 22
Mahbub Ali, Syed 174
Mahdi Hasan Nasiri 153
Mahmud Ahmad Hunar 155
Mahmud, Syed **92**, 119, 120
Malacca jail 98, 99
Malaviya, Keshav Dev 100
Malaviya, Krishnakant 100
Malaviya, Madan Mohan 94, **94**, 96, 98, 99, 122
Malaviya, Padmakant 98, 99
Manmohan Das (Bachcha-ji) 27, 82, 124
Manohar Das 27
Manzar Ali Sokhta 98
Markandeya 113
Mauryas 12, 20, 49
 Ashoka 20, **20**, 49, **50**, 54, 55
 Chandragupta 20, 38
Mears, Grimwood 123
Mehrotra, K.K. **104**, 134
Mehta, J.K. 134
Mehta, Pherozeshah 96
Minto Park 54, **80**, 94
Mirza Ghulam 58, 59, **60**, 62, 68
Mirza Kalb-e Husain Khan Nadir 152
Mishra, Brijesh Kumar 27
Mishra, Santosh Kumar 27
Mishrilal 27
Mitter, Julien 134

Mittra, Dr 103, 104
Mohan Lal 134
Moti Mahal Talkies **107**
Mughals 11, 45, 46, 48, 53, 54, 61–63, 69–71, 73, 89, 115, 121, 124, 130, 148, 174, 175
 Akbar **6**, 7, 15, 22, 24, 25, **44**, 45–55, **45**, 57–61, 65, 68, 73
 Dara Shikoh **147**, 148, 171
 Jahangir/Salim 46, 49, **50**, 52–54, 56–71
 Khusrau **50**, 52, **52–54**, 53, 57
 Nur Jahan **50**
 Shah Alam II 46, **46**, 54, 150
 Shahjahan/Khurram 45, 46, 69
Muhammad Afzal Sabit 149
Muhammad Ajmal, Shah 150, 151
Muhammad Alim Betab, Shah 152
Muhammad Alim, Syed 152
Muhammad Azim Sabat 149
Muhammad Nasir Afzali, Shah 149, 150
Muhammad Qannauji, Syed 148
Muhammad Tahir, Shah 148
Muhammad Taqi Mir, Mir 147
Muhammad Yahya, Shah 148, 152
Muhibbullah Ilahabadi, Shah 147, **147**, 148, **149**, 152
Muir College **6**, 81, 103, 115, 121, 128–30, **130**, 133, **135**, **136**, 137, 139, 153, 167
Muirabad 82
Mujtaba Husain 155
Mukhopadhyaya, Subhash 160
Mulla, Anand Narain 155
Mulla, Jagat Narain 121
Mumfordgunj 84
Municipal Gazette 84
Municipality 78, 84, 159, 171
Muzaffar Hasan, Sayyad 169

Nagas **33**, 36, **36**, 37, 41
Naga-Vasuki/Temple 12, **14**, **15**, 31, 35, **36**
Naidu, P.S.V. 134
Naini/jail 27, 81, 99, **144**, 157, 174
Naoroji, Dadabhai 94
Narayan, Jai Prakash 99, 163, 174
Narendra Dev, Acharya 99
Nasikh, Imam Bakhsh 150
Naubat Rai Nazar 155
Naval Kishore Press 139
Naye Patte 113
Nayee Kavita 113
Nazeer Ali Zaidi, Sayyad 169
Nazir Ahmad, Maulvi 153
Nehru, Jawaharlal 39, 84, **94**, 96, 98, 100, **100**, 101, 103–05, **117**, 121, 141, 145, 156–65, **159**, **165**, 171, 172
Nehru, Motilal 82, **92**, **94**, 96, 98, **98**, 99, **99**, 122–24, **124**
Nigam, Khush-hal Chandra 174
Nikash 113
Nirala, Suryakant Tripathi 103, 140, 141, **141**, 144
Niranjanis 37

Nirvanis **30**
Nurul Absar 155

Pajawa 26
Pal, Bipin Chandra 94
Palace Theatre **78**
Pande, Govind Chand 133
Pandit, Vijayalakshmi **124**, 159
Pant, Govind Ballabh 99, 158, **158**
Pant, Sumitranandan 107, 113, 139–42, **142**, 144
Parimal Group 111, 113, 141, 143
Parkes, Fanny 73
Pasis 91, 92
Patalpuri Temple **8**, **11**, **13**, 15,
Patel, Ramadheen 100
Patel, Vallabhbhai 157, 158, **158**
Patharchatti **24**, 25, 26
Phaphamau/Bridge 28, 90
(The) Pioneer **74**, 81, 99, 129
 Old Pioneer Press **74**
Plowden, Chichele 117
Pragatisheel Lekhak Sangh 143
Prasads 121
Pratapgarh 87, 92
Prayag Mahila Vidyapeeth 141
Prayag Sangeet Samiti 77
Prayagraj **11**
Prayagwals 39
Premchand, Munshi **152**, 154, 155
Presbyterians 74, 81
Prince of Wales 100, 128
Progressive Writers' Association 111, 113, 141, 143, 144, 154, 155

Rajendra Prasad **97**
Ramanujis 38
Ram-dal **23**, **24**, 26, 27
Ramlila/Ramkatha 25–28, **25**
Ranade, Mahadev Govind 134
Rani Mandi 26, 82, **171**, 172
Raza, Rahi Masoom 164
Richard Sahib 89
Robinson, Julian **74**
Rudra, S.K. 84

Sada Sukh Lal 155
Saha, Meghnad 133
Sahi, V.D.N. 113
Sajjad Zaheer, Syed 154
Sakir 174
Sangam **6**, 14, 22, **35**, 37, 38, **38**, 40, **40**, 157, **157**, 158
Sangram Singh 90–92
Sapru, Tej Bahadur 82, 122, 124, 155
Sara Seward Memorial Hospital 81
Saraswati 140, **140**, 142
Saraswati, river 11, 14, 31, 35
Sarojini Naidu Marg 78, **115**, 116
Saxena, Sarveshvar Dayal 113
Sen, Surendranath 96, 121
Shafaat Ahmad Khan 133
Shah Begum **50**, 52, 53
Shahabpur 90, 91, 100
Shahid Hussain, Sheikh 174
Shahkar 155

Shaikh/Shah Muhammad Afzal 148
Shakir, Pyare Lal 155
Shanti Narayan 99, 100
Sharma, G.R. 133
Shastri, Lal Bahadur 101, **101**, 157, **159**, **160**
Shivkoti ghat 26
Shukla, Madhav 98
Shultankeshwara Temple 14
Simeons 121
Singh, V.P. 101, **169**, 174
Sinha, Durganand 133
Sinha, J.M.L. 124
Sinha, Sachchidanand 99, 120
South Road 78
Srinath Singh 99
Sringaverapura **6**, **17**, 26, **26**
Sripat Rai 142
St Joseph's Collegiate 81
St Mary's Convent 79, 81
St Thomas's Church **6**
Stanley Road 77
Sultan Nisar Begum **50**, 53
Swaraj Bhavan **92**, 103
Swarajya 99

Taimni, I.K. 134
Tambolan's tomb 53, 54
Tandon, P.D. 98, 99, 158, **159**
Tara Chand 153
Thibaut, Professor 130, 133
Thornhill-Mayne Library 77, **82–85**, 85, 103
Tilak, Lokmanya 94
Tiwari, Venkatesh Narayan 99
Tripathi, R.P. 133
Tudball, William 117

Uprising of 1857 54, 77, 87–90, **87**, **90**, 92, 116, 129

Vaheed Ilahabadi 153
Vaid, Krishna Baldev 139, **140**
Vaqar Azim, Syed 155
Varma, Bhagwati Charan 107, 108, 144
Varma, Lakshmi Kant 113
Varma, Mahadevi 107, 140, 141, **142**, 144
Verma, Ram Kumar 133
Victoria, Queen 75, **80**, 94, **123**
Vishwambhar Palace Talkies **108**

Williams, Rushbrook 133

Xuanzang 15, 20, 22, **26**, 38, 39

Yahyagunj 148
Yamuna, river **6**, 11, 12, 14, 15, 18, 24, 31, 48, 49, 52, 54, 73, 74, 157

Zair, Shah Muhammad Fakhir 148, 150
Zakaullah, Maulvi 15

Contributors

Neelum Saran Gour, guest editor of this volume, is Professor of English at the University of Allahabad, and a fiction writer. She has published six books, including *Speaking of '62* (1995), *Sikandar Chowk Park* (2005), and *Messres Dickens, Doyle and Wodehouse* (2005). Her forthcoming books include *Baasath ki Baatein*, a Hindi translation of *Speaking of '62*. She has been writing a column on Allahabad, and was writer-in-residence at the University of Kent, UK, and at Jawaharlal Nehru University, New Delhi.

Arindam Roy is the Managing Editor of an online Citizen Journalists' portal, Merinews (www.merinews.com). He has worked with *Himmat*, *Economic and Political Weekly*, *Sundaram*, *The Northern India Patrika*, *The Times of India*, Allahabad, and *Hindustan Times*, Allahabad and Varanasi. He has co-authored *Kumbh Mela, Indian Pilgrimage* (2001).

N.R. Farooqi has an MA in Medieval History from the University of Allahabad and a PhD from the University of Wisconsin, USA. He has published three books and a number of articles in national and international journals and has held several international fellowships. He is Professor of History and Dean, Faculty of Arts, University of Allahabad.

Asok Kumar Das, well known to readers of *Marg*, specializes in Mughal art. Currently he is an Andrew W. Mellon Fellow working on Ustad Mansur and Mughal Natural History Drawings at the Metropolitan Museum of Art, New York.

John Bennett Harrison read History at Cambridge and did war service in India. He later secured a post in Indian History at London University (SOAS) which he held from 1947 to 1982. Two research years were spent at Allahabad investigating the planning and building of the Civil Lines and the city's functioning social, administrative, and economic systems and the role of the local Indian service communities. He lives in Hereford, England.

Badri Narayan Tiwari is Lecturer in Social History and Anthropology at Govind Ballabh Pant Social Science Institute, Jhunsi. He is also in charge of the Manav Vikas Sangrahalaya and the Dalit Resource Centre of the Institute's Centre for Culture, Power and Change. He has been a Fellow at the University Grants Commission, Indian Council for Historical Research, New Delhi, and Indian Institute of Advanced Studies, Shimla, and has held international fellowships.

Hemendra Shankar Saxena taught at Allahabad University from 1948 until 1988. He was a British Council scholar in London in 1959–60 researching 20th-century fiction with special reference to D.H. Lawrence. He has written extensively on the city of Allahabad in both Hindi and English.

Manas Mukul Das taught at the University of Allahabad from 1964 until 2002. He was awarded the Distinguished Teacher Award for the year 2000. He is the author of *Thomas Hardy – Poet of Tragic Vision* (1983). He is now involved in a project for alternative holistic education.

Harish Trivedi is Professor of English at the University of Delhi and has been Visiting Professor at the Universities of Chicago and London. He is the author of *Colonial Transactions: English Literature and India* (1993, 1995). He has translated from Hindi *Premchand: His Life and Times* (1982), and contributed a chapter on "Hindi and the Nation" to *Literary Cultures in History: Reconstructions from South Asia*, ed. Sheldon Pollock (2003, 2004) and on "Ilahabad aur Banaras" to *Kalpana: Kashi Ank*, ed. Prayag Shukla (2005).

Shamsur Rahman Faruqi spent a large part of his life in the Indian Civil Service. He has also been Adjunct Professor at the South Asia Center in the University of Pennsylvania, and Khan Abdul Ghaffar Khan Professor in the Faculty of Humanities at Jamia Millia University, New Delhi. He is widely regarded as the chief theorist of literary modernism in Urdu. Among his other areas of expertise are 18th-century Urdu poetry and early Urdu literary culture and history. His novel *Ka'i Chand the Sar-e Asman* (2006) was published in both India and Pakistan, to universal acclaim.

Gangeya Mukherji is a Fellow at the Indian Institute of Advanced Study, Shimla, working on a project titled, "The Philosophy of Integration and Reconciliation" which has particular reference to the thought of Gandhi and Tagore. He has contributed many research papers to journals such as *Studies in Humanities and Social Sciences*, *Mainstream*, and *Seminar*.

Rajesh Vora is an independent photographer with a strong interest in the documentary tradition of photography.